Comprehension
That *Works*

Taking Students Beyond Ordinary Understanding to Deep Comprehension

Authors
Danny Brassell, Ph.D. and Timothy Rasinski, Ph.D.
Foreword by Hallie Yopp, Ph.D.

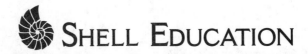

SHELL EDUCATION

Comprehension That Works
Taking Students Beyond Ordinary Understanding to Deep Comprehension

Editors
Joan Irwin, M.A
Wendy Conklin, M.A.

Assistant Editor
Leslie Huber, M.A.

Editorial Director
Lori Kamola, M.S.Ed

Editor-in-Chief
Sharon Coan, M.S.Ed.

Editorial Manager
Gisela Lee, M.A.

Creative Director
Lee Aucoin

Print Production Manager
Don Tran

Interior Layout Designer
Robin Erickson

Print Production
Juan Chavolla
Phil Garcia

Publisher
Corinne Burton, M.A.Ed.

Shell Education
5301 Oceanus Drive
Huntington Beach, CA 92649
http://www.shelleducation.com
ISBN 978-1-4258-0264-6
© *2008 Shell Educational Publishing, Inc.*
Reprinted 2010

Table of Contents

Chapter 9: Comprehension Strategies for After Reading

Foreword

One of the most significant gifts we can offer our students is the ability to read. Reading opens worlds of possibility. It empowers. It transforms. It liberates. Readers can peer into and ponder the minds and hearts of others. Readers can explore the past and consider the future. They can seek information and find inspiration. The benefits of reading are beyond measure. Those who choose to be teachers have chosen to participate in the profoundly important task of ensuring that our students become readers. Teachers have an incredible responsibility.

Fortunately, Danny Brassell and Timothy Rasinski have teamed to write a practical and timely text for teachers that focuses on the heart of reading. They understand, and help teachers understand, that reading is not just saying the words on a page. It is not merely a matter of decoding smoothly and with expression. It is not simply the ability to respond to low-level questions about the content of a text selection. They impress upon us that reading is a thoughtful process that involves deep comprehension. It is this deep comprehension that empowers, transforms, and liberates readers. It is what we *must*, as educators, hold at the fore of our teaching. It is the *why* we must keep in mind as we plan our reading instruction and engage with our students.

Comprehension That Works: Taking Students Beyond Ordinary Understanding to Deep Comprehension succinctly summarizes many important understandings in our field about reading development. It shares research-based insights about motivation, differentiation, and strategic reading. It reminds us how proficient readers read, and it reviews the complexities of reading difficulties. It provides, in a friendly and accessible manner, the theoretical and empirical bases for effective reading comprehension instruction.

Readers of this text will welcome the many practical and easily implemented teaching strategies that Brassell and Rasinski share. As you peruse the text, you will recognize that the authors—academics and authorities in their fields—have spent time with students. Brassell and Rasinski obviously have a wealth of experience with readers of all ages and abilities. Their suggestions are clearly grounded in the "real world" of teaching. Teachers will find their suggestions relevant and realistic. Most importantly, teachers will discover that they can support deep comprehension.

I am confident that teachers will find this text valuable and will read it carefully. As they do so, they will question, they will make connections, they will imagine their own students engaging in the strategies. They will comprehend deeply, and they will be inspired to pass this ability on to our students. Thanks, Danny! Thanks, Tim!

Hallie Kay Yopp, Ph.D.

Preface

A little over 10 years ago, I submitted my first academic article to the International Reading Association's elementary school journal, *The Reading Teacher*. The article was accepted, and I received a nice note of encouragement from the journal's editor, Tim Rasinski. Since then, Tim has acted as a mentor to me, and we have exchanged a variety of teaching ideas during our encounters on the road speaking at various venues. One of the recurring topics we have discussed has been collaborating on a book, as we share a common concern: how do we write a book that is research based, practical for teachers, and interesting to read?

Without sufficient time to plan their curricula and meet the standards set by local, state, and federal officials, more and more teachers are seeking ways to integrate curricula in ways that interest students, while satisfying school-district mandates. Many education books tend to overwhelm readers with educational theories or offer teachers practical ideas with little substance. In the spirit of other professional resources offered by Shell Education, we wanted to create a book for those teachers who need a lot of useful, standards-based strategies that they can implement immediately without the need for extensive training or materials. We believe we can offer teachers a resource that goes beyond ordinary comprehension.

Comprehension That Works: Taking Students Beyond Ordinary Understanding to Deep Comprehension focuses on how teachers can utilize unique and engaging classroom-tested, research-based comprehension strategies that meet all standards. We waste no time in establishing the theoretical foundations of such a program, explaining why these comprehension strategies matter, and suggesting how to facilitate comprehension activities that utilize and benefit students' multiple intelligences.

Reading comprehension requires motivation, mental frameworks for holding ideas, concentration, active engagement, and good study techniques. Our book provides practical, research-based guidelines for reading comprehension instruction in grades K–6 that meet standards without sacrificing student (or teacher) interest. The book integrates current research findings with real-life observations of effective teachers and diverse students in action, identifying the strategies that successful readers use to comprehend many different types of materials. Recommendations are offered for organizing the classroom effectively and planning instruction to broaden each student's repertoire of comprehension strategies. Additionally, concrete, classroom-tested approaches are described to help students engage with fiction and nonfiction texts, develop their vocabularies, build study and test-taking skills, and become motivated, lifelong readers.

We hope that by including numerous sample activities, lesson and center ideas, as well as assessment tools, classroom teachers will feel less overwhelmed by comprehension standards and empowered to facilitate innovative and engaging instruction with their students. Our hope is that this book will encourage teachers to extend learning beyond ordinary comprehension toward deep comprehension.

Danny Brassell, Ph.D., and Timothy Rasinski, Ph.D.

Introduction

In this book, we describe effective reading comprehension strategies based on our experiences as teachers and observers of outstanding teachers. Our aim is to provide teachers with a body of comprehension strategies that challenge students to think about textual meanings at deep levels of understanding; the theoretical and evidence-based support for the comprehension strategies presented in the session; and rich, contextualized descriptions of the comprehension strategies in actual classroom and clinical settings with students and teachers.

Comprehension is the essential goal of reading and reading instruction. Effective comprehension instruction goes beyond literal comprehension by challenging students to make deep inferences about texts, to think critically about the material they read, and to creatively transform the texts they encounter into other forms and formats. Moreover, effective instruction in comprehension should be engaging for students and teachers. That is, instruction should be designed in ways that challenge students to think creatively and to display their creative thinking to work in ways that are engaging, authentic, and enjoyable, and in which they can take justifiable pride. Effective comprehension instruction should provide teachers with tools for differentiating instruction for all students, whether they are gifted, struggling, or English language learners.

In each chapter of this book, we share instructional comprehension strategies that satisfy the instructional needs and principles identified in the previous paragraph—strategies that are effective and go beyond the ordinary. These strategies are based on solid research and theory in comprehension processing, as well as our own classroom and reading clinic experience with students and teachers.

In Chapter 1, we define reading comprehension, examine its importance, and present an overview of the increasing body of research that has formed over the past 30 years in favor of reading comprehension support. Chapter 2 offers ways to get students excited about reading. We discuss the characteristics of proficient readers in Chapter 3. In Chapter 4, we examine how to assess students' reading comprehension (e.g., prior knowledge of various texts, topics, and strategies). In Chapter 5, we examine ways that teachers can differentiate comprehension instruction to meet the needs of all students. Chapter 6 reviews a number of other strategies teachers may use to build their students' comprehension skills. Finally, Chapters 7–9 examine a variety of strategies teachers may use to strengthen students' comprehension of texts before, during, and after reading. *You're the Expert* is a feature that invites you to think about your beliefs and practices regarding teaching reading. *At Your Fingertips* provides suggestions for teaching resources and professional reflection, as well as short summaries of research relevant to comprehension instruction.

Some of the strategies in this book will be familiar to teachers. Other strategies in this book may seem a bit different from what teachers have used or encountered in the past. These lesser-known comprehension strategies may tap into the interests and needs of students who may not otherwise find reading easy or fulfilling. These are strategies that have been used with students at the Reading and Writing Center at Kent State University and have been found to be effective and engaging. Classroom teachers have also used these strategies with students and have found them valuable in drawing students' attention to the meaning of what they read. What is offered in this volume expands the notion of what counts as effective comprehension instruction. Comprehension instruction can be much more than simply asking students questions at the end of a reading or having them respond to what they have read by writing a summary or completing an activity sheet. Comprehension instruction can and should be effective, but it should also be engaging and creative, and tap into the various talents and gifts of all students.

What Is Reading? What Is Reading Comprehension?

On a bright fall morning on the campus of Kent State University in Ohio, student clinicians in the university's Reading and Writing Center are gearing up to assess and diagnose the reading of several children referred to the center because of reading difficulties experienced in school and at home. One of the diagnostic teams is assigned Marcus, a bright-eyed third grader, who is more than pleased to have the undivided attention of the three adults who have been assigned to work with him. After meeting Marcus and asking him to share with them his interests in and attitudes about reading, the clinicians have Marcus read orally some passages from an informal reading inventory.

Marcus is eager to do so. However, before beginning to read the first passage, he asks the clinicians an interesting question: "Should I read the stories as fast as I can?" The clinicians are momentarily taken aback but recover quickly to remind him to read in his best voice in order to understand what he reads. They remind him that they will be asking him to retell what he has read after reading each passage.

Despite the reminder, Marcus reads the first passage quickly and with remarkable accuracy—only one word-recognition error. However, he pays little attention to punctuation and demonstrates very little expression in his oral reading. Moreover, when he is asked to retell what he has just read, he struggles to provide even a few accurate memories of the passage. Still, he ends this first reading with a smile on his face; clearly he feels that he has impressed the clinicians with his reading.

Natalia, another third grader from a different school in the same town, arrives at the Reading and Writing Center a few minutes later with her parents. Although she is a bit more reticent than Marcus, she also eases into the morning of reading with another set of clinicians assigned to assess and diagnose her reading. Natalia is asked to read orally some graded passages from an informal reading inventory. Natalia asks no questions before beginning to read. Her reading is slow and labored, and she makes several errors in recognizing words; but she perseveres and makes it to the end of the first passage.

When asked to retell what she has read, Natalia's demeanor changes from an intense reader focused on making it through the text to a child who is able to quickly provide a detailed recollection of nearly every event from the passage she has just read. Moreover, in her retelling, she notes how she has had some of the same experiences in her own life that were described in the reading. She even noted how she felt during those experiences.

The clinical teams continued to work with Marcus and Natalia throughout the morning and were able to identify their strengths and difficulties in order to provide parents and teachers with recommendations for helping the children overcome those difficulties. Both children left the reading center that morning tired, but with smiles on their faces.

You're the Expert

Both Marcus and Natalia struggle with reading, yet they each manifest different behaviors while reading and retelling what they have read. How do you think Marcus views reading? How would he define *reading*? What do you think Natalia thinks about reading? Who is the better reader? Why do you think so?

Reading is a multidimensional process that involves the eyes, the ears, the mouth, and most importantly, the brain. What counts for you as reading? Consider the following tasks:

1. How would you describe or define *reading* to a child or person who doesn't know how to read? What are the most essential elements of reading?

2. Find two children and ask them how they would describe or define *reading* to someone who doesn't read.

Consider your response and the responses of the children. What are the essential elements of reading? Do the responses vary at all? What do these responses tell you about how reading is viewed by people?

To most reading specialists, the one essential element involved in reading is making meaning. In other words, turning those written squiggles on a page into meaningful thoughts, not just those expressed by the author, but also those that are triggered in the reader as he or she reads. These thoughts may even go beyond the content expressed in the text itself. Reading is the creation of meaning from the printed page. Although it may involve the sounding out of words, accessing the meaning of words, reading the text with appropriate fluency, and providing expression, these are all sideshows to the main event—making meaning.

Reading and Reading Comprehension

At its heart, *reading* refers to the ability to comprehend or make meaning from written text. A dictionary definition of the word *read* states that it is the ability to examine and comprehend the meaning of written words. Comprehension, then, is at the heart of any conventional definition of reading.

Comprehension and reading comprehension, however, are concepts that, to a certain degree, defy specific definition. What does it mean to *comprehend*? Some might say comprehension is the act of understanding. That brings up the question: what is understanding? The dictionary says that *comprehension* is the ability to know or grasp ideas with the mind. Indeed, the term *comprehend* is derived from the Latin *prehendere* which means "to grasp." Again, however, these words that are used to define the term *comprehension* are as vague as the term *comprehension* itself. How does one know when an idea is fully grasped? How does one demonstrate full comprehension or knowledge of ideas? Does a mere retelling of what one reads, as is done in some tests of reading comprehension, demonstrate adequate comprehension? The notion of *grasping* suggests that there is an action required of the reader in order to grasp the meaning of the text. Reading comprehension is not a passive activity in which meaning "magically" appears once the reader reads the words in the text.

Reading and literacy scholars have created their own definitions of reading comprehension that contain a bit more precision. Reading comprehension is the construction of the meaning of a written communication through a reciprocal, holistic interchange of ideas between the interpreter and the message (Harris and Hodges 1995, 39). The presumption is that meaning resides in the intentional problem-solving and thinking processes of the interpreter. The content of meaning is influenced by that person's prior knowledge and experience.

This definition also suggests that reading comprehension requires an action on the part of the reader. That action involves the use of the existing knowledge that the reader has on the topic of the text as well as the text itself in order to create meaning. The problem in reading comprehension is making meaning from the text. The problem is solved by the intentional action of the reader, which includes the purpose for reading as well as the ability to draw upon prior knowledge that is relevant to the text. The question now becomes, what types of actions do readers engage in that allow them to solve the problem of making meaning from the text?

Three-Level Taxonomy of Comprehension

Thomas Barrett has suggested the following three types of action with his three-level taxonomy of reading comprehension (Clymer 1968).

Literal Comprehension: Literal comprehension, the lowest of the three levels, requires a reader to be able to retell or recall the facts or information presented in a text. Names of characters and details of the setting are examples of literal comprehension. The information required for literal comprehension comes largely from the text itself. Recall comprehension can easily be evaluated. In responding to a literal question, the reader either can recall the information from the text or he or she cannot.

Inferential Comprehension: Inferential comprehension, the next level, refers to the ability of a reader to take in information that is inferred or implied within a text. If a text indicates that a character is carrying an umbrella while walking down a street on a cloudy day, you can infer that the character is expecting rain. Inferential comprehension is more sophisticated than literal comprehension because it requires the orchestration and manipulation of information from the text as well as information that resides within the readers—their background knowledge.

Critical Comprehension: Critical or evaluative comprehension, the third and highest level in the taxonomy, involves making critical judgments about the information presented in the text. Were the characters reputable and honest in their actions? Did the selection offer the reader new information, new insights, or added enjoyment? Were the characters authentic? Was the literary quality of the text high? Answers to such questions require a high level of interaction between information from the text, the reader, perhaps other people with whom the reader has interacted, or even other texts the reader has read. Moreover, in-depth analysis and critical thinking are necessary to make informed judgments and evaluations. Because responses to inferential and critical-level questions are highly dependent on the reader's own background, interest, and disposition, determining a reader's level and the quality of a reader's inferential and critical comprehension is not easy.

All three levels of comprehension are important and need to be fostered. However, it has generally been the case that inferential and critical comprehension are not sufficiently addressed in many classrooms and reading programs. These levels are not easily evaluated and do not lend themselves to the "teacher asks and student answers" type of comprehension discussions that follow many reading lessons. Nevertheless, a focus on inferential and critical comprehension is appropriate, and nurtures the high-level thinking that one would expect to find in high-performing classrooms.

Transformational Model of Comprehension

Reading comprehension is the ability to take information from written text and do something with it in a way that demonstrates knowledge or understanding of that information. Comprehension occurs when a reader is able to act on, respond to, or transform the information that is presented in written text in ways that demonstrate understanding. The following examples illustrate how readers can show they understand what they read.

When a reader is able to engage in an intelligent discussion about a text with others, the reader is demonstrating comprehension of the passage. When a reader is able to relate text to real events, the reader is demonstrating comprehension. When a reader is able to apply information from a text to a new situation, such as fixing an automobile, the reader is demonstrating comprehension. When a reader is able to transform a narrative story into a poem, play, newspaper article, critical review, insightful essay, entertaining advertisement, visual image, musical score, or dance movement, the reader is demonstrating a sophisticated level of understanding of text.

Comprehension demands that readers do something with a text beyond simple verbatim retelling of the information from the text itself. A reader needs to take the information from the text and transform it in some way, using his or her own thought processes in order to comprehend and demonstrate comprehension of what he or she has read. This is called the transformational model of reading comprehension. The activities we describe in this book are based on this model and are designed to engage students in purposeful and meaningful reading experiences.

A Processing Definition of Reading

Another approach to defining reading comes from the work of the National Reading Panel (NRP). The NRP is a group of literacy experts commissioned by the federal government in the 1990s to examine current and past research on literacy acquisition and identify factors associated with success in learning to read. The panel identified five factors that could be thought of as essential components of reading and learning to read (National Reading Panel 2000):

Factor 1: Phonemic awareness refers to the ability to conceptualize, think about, and manipulate the sounds of language.

Factor 2: Phonics or decoding refers to the ability to translate the written symbols used in reading (i.e., letters) into sounds and orally produced words.

Factor 3: Vocabulary is the ability of readers to grasp the meaning of individual words and phrases used in written texts.

Factor 4: Fluency refers to two distinct competencies. First, fluency is the ability to process the printed text so automatically and effortlessly that a reader can devote a maximal amount of his or her attention to constructing the meaning of the author's message. The second aspect of fluency is the ability to read a text orally, with expression that reflects the syntactic and semantic nature of the written text.

The first four of these components do not directly deal with meaning, but they are necessary conditions that allow readers to focus on comprehension. So, while these four components are not equal to comprehension, a proficiency in these areas most certainly assists students with the comprehension of text.

Factor 5: The fifth component identified by the NRP is comprehension. The panel identified seven types of comprehension instruction, or comprehension processes, that enable readers to grasp or make meaning from written text. All seven are supported by scientific evidence that has demonstrated that when teachers use these processes or teach them to students, students are more likely to comprehend or make meaning from what they read. These comprehension processes correspond well with the actions required of a reader to respond to and/or transform texts, which were mentioned earlier in this chapter. The comprehension processes identified by the panel include:

- **Graphic and semantic organizers**—The use of graphic representations of written material can aid readers in making meaning.

- **Question answering**—Readers are more likely to understand what they read when they are asked questions about the reading by their teacher and receive immediate feedback about their answers.

- **Question generation**—Readers are more likely to understand what they read when they ask questions of themselves about various aspects of their reading before and during the reading itself.

- **Text structure**—Helping readers understand the underlying organization or structure of a written text has been found to aid them in understanding and recalling the information from the passage.

- **Summarization**—Readers are better able to understand what they read when they engage in distilling, integrating, and generalizing the information from a passage into its key ideas in the form of a brief summary.

- **Cooperative learning**—Students are more likely to make meaning from a text when they engage in the process of making meaning with other students.

- **Comprehension monitoring**—Successful comprehenders monitor or are aware of their own comprehension and make strategic decisions to employ certain strategies or processes, depending on how successful they feel they are in making meaning from their reading.

Research exists that supports the use of these strategies and processes to improve reading comprehension. A common thread in each of these strategies is that they actively engage the reader in making and monitoring meaning from the text. Readers must get the mental gears in their heads turning to make comprehension happen. These strategies require readers to make their mental gears turn.

Although these strategies have been shown to be effective, their identification by the National Reading Panel does not imply that these are the only strategies that are useful in teaching reading comprehension. Any comprehension strategy that requires students to engage in thoughtful, deliberative discussion about the text they are reading will foster understanding.

Chapter 2

Engaging Student Interest

Gonzalo traced an invisible line on the carpet with his left index finger while humming a tune he heard on his father's car radio this past weekend. Miriam whispered something in Jessica's ear that united the two in a quiet giggle. Ephraim threw another piece of floor lint at Luis, despite Sara's disapproving grimaces and nudges. Tyrell simply rocked back and forth, anxious to raise his hand and share a story.

This is the teacher's first year, and Tyrell knew it. He knew it because the principal told the class on the first day of school to be nice to the teacher because he had never taught anybody before. Belinda said that their teacher looks too young to teach, and Tyrell agreed. Tyrell is supposed to be nice, though, because his mama said his new teacher is cute.

The young teacher stood before his class of second graders, most of whom possessed limited English proficiency, and recited a story from one of two language arts textbooks that the school provided his class of 33 students. The teacher's mentor said that although the text is designed to be a 10-minute read-aloud, he can probably read it to the class in five or six minutes…if he reads quickly, skips questions, and ignores students' comments. The comprehension exercise, the mentor assured him, should not take too long. After sneaking a peek at his students' expressions, the young teacher agreed with his mentor. The comprehension exercise should not take too long because hardly any students were paying attention.

How can teachers expect students to comprehend the stories that they read or the stories teachers read aloud to them if the students have no interest in the reading selections? Before students can comprehend what they read, they need to understand why they are reading it and participate in a classroom environment that caters to their interests. This chapter will offer ways to get students excited about reading.

You're the Expert

1. What could the young teacher do to engage his or her students in the read-aloud?

2. Think of a time when you were disengaged as a student. What could the teacher have done to captivate your attention?

3. The young teacher above is one of the authors, Danny Brassell, during his first year of teaching. He admitted that it took him time to get his feet wet before he understood how to balance curricular standards and district mandates with the interests of his students. With the support of colleagues, Danny observed talented veteran teachers and recollected approaches used by his favorite teachers when he was a student in order to improve his classroom environment. Think back to your own experiences as a beginning teacher and how you have changed over the course of your career. How have colleagues helped you? How have you helped beginning teachers?

4. List three to five ways to create a classroom that engages students' interests in reading.

Numerous factors play a role in students' comprehension of a text. Is the text developmentally appropriate and written at students' reading comfort level? What is students' background knowledge of the items, issues, events, and people discussed in the text? Are students familiar with the structure of the text (e.g., business letter, newspaper article, reading textbook, how-to manual)?

Attention plays a major role in students' comprehension. A topic may seem fascinating to a teacher, but if that topic has little to do with the interests and experiences of the students, their comprehension may suffer. Effective teachers can bring any subject to life for students. They do this, however, by relating subjects to students' interests and prior experiences. Reading comprehension declines when students are not actively engaged with a text.

Newspapers demonstrate the power of actively engaging readers on a daily basis. For example, news stories and advertisements captivate readers' interests because readers are trying to learn new information. For those more interested in emotional pieces, feature stories and columns focus less on statistics and events and more on how those occurrences affect individuals.

At Your Fingertips

Newspapers are an excellent resource for teachers who want to engage the diverse interests of their students. When Danny taught in an under-resourced area, he relied on newspapers out of necessity to ensure that his students had a variety of materials to read. Some teachers today may find themselves in a similar situation. Newspapers can be lifesavers, as they are easily accessible, plentiful, and usually free. Brassell (2007) describes multiple benefits of using newspapers in the classroom, including the following:

1. Newspapers offer something for each student's individual interests, from sports to news to diagrams to movie times.

2. Students can take newspapers home.

3. Teaching students to read newspapers daily builds reading habits that last a lifetime.

4. Newspapers offer students models for a large variety of writing styles.

For additional information on strategies to use with newspapers in building your students' comprehension skills, check out *News Flash! Newspaper Activities to Meet Language Arts Standards and Differentiate Instruction* (Brassell 2007). Many schools participate in Newspaper in Education (NIE) programs sponsored by papers in various locations throughout the country. These programs include materials for both teachers and students. The Newspaper Association of America Foundation, the organization that administers NIE programs, is a source for more information (see http://www.naafoundation.org/NewspaperInEducation.aspx.). Additionally, you will find it helpful to check with your local newspaper about resources and opportunities to participate in NIE programs.

Think back to when you were a child. What are your favorite memories of learning to read? How did you learn to read? This question has been asked of thousands of adults, and rarely does a person fondly recall good times spent on grandpa's lap as he drilled sounds of letters. It is not that phonics instruction does not have a place in reading instruction. On the contrary, explicit phonics instruction is an essential element of a good reading program. In fact, the National Reading Panel (2000) identified phonics as one of the five essential components of reading. While comprehension also made that list, and members of the panel agreed that comprehension is the ultimate goal of reading, the panel omitted a key sixth component—motivation. Before students can comprehend what they are reading, they must first be engaged in what they are reading.

Guthrie and Cox (2001) identified seven important features of a classroom context that fosters long-term reading engagement:

1. learning and knowledge goals

2. real-world interaction

3. interesting texts

4. autonomy support

5. strategy instruction

6. collaboration support

7. evaluation

The rest of this chapter will discuss the strategies that classroom teachers can use to engage students' reading interests.

Learning and Knowledge Goals

Able readers are active readers who understand that comprehension is the goal of reading. Davis (2007) observes "students who are able to comprehend a variety of texts will be able to integrate comprehension strategies according to the kind of text they are reading. These students will be able to explain what they are doing when they comprehend and what they do when they realize that they do not comprehend" (189–190). Instruction that promotes active and challenging engagement with text will benefit all students. Effective reading lessons begin with the teacher and students talking together about purposes for reading and sharing observations about personal experiences related to the topic of the text. This discussion provides a setting in which the teacher can help students focus on concepts in the text, as well as alerting them to skills they may need to apply as they read. These preliminary activities ensure that specific skills and concepts are not taught in isolation.

One of the best ways to improve students' comprehension of any reading selection is to organize reading and language arts time around a specific theme. By grouping specific strategies and skills into one theme, teachers help students expand their expertise with that theme. Students can read a variety of books, poems, songs, articles, and other reading materials to solidify their understanding of a theme. Teachers may even integrate a reading and language arts theme into other curricular areas to focus students' attention.

Effective teachers engage their students by building upon students' prior experiences. The best way to earn students' attention is to relate materials to their interests. To do this, however, teachers first need to become familiar with their students' prior experiences.

By brainstorming what students already know about a subject, teachers are better equipped to develop lessons that will not bore students with information that they already know or with material well above their level. When teachers determine what students know and what they want to know, students become more engaged in their reading and achieve a higher level of success.

Donna Ogle (1986) developed KWL+ charts for teachers to graphically organize students' background knowledge about a topic and to assist them in organizing questions to guide them in their learning. It requires students to focus on four questions: what they know (K), what they want to know (W), what they learned (L), and what they still want to learn more about (+). The strategy is used to engage students' interest in reading by making them active participants and to clarify their purpose for reading by constantly encouraging them to ask themselves questions. Realizing and understanding their purpose for reading helps students understand how reading relates to the "real world."

Real-World Interaction

"Why do we need to learn this?" is a battle cry heard throughout classrooms across America. Students constantly want to know from teachers how they will use what they learn in the classroom out in the real world.

Once teachers develop a better understanding of their students' prior experiences and background knowledge, they can better influence the reading comprehension of their students. By allowing students to share their own personal experiences and realia, teachers can plan lessons that build on students' understanding and beliefs. Allowing students to "experience" a text also aids in their comprehension. Examples of this would include writing journals, narratives, or poems about various concepts.

Double-entry journals, for example, allow students to reflect on what they read and relate it to their own lives (Barone 1990). A double-entry journal is simply a paper divided vertically in half to provide two thin columns. (Sometimes teachers tell their students to fold the paper like a hot dog, not like a hamburger which would result in two wide, stubby columns.) On the left-hand side of the page, students write quotes or transcribe short informational passages from the book or other text they are reading and write their reactions on the right-hand side of the page. An uncomplicated and straightforward process, double-entry journals are a powerful way for students to relate interesting things that they read to their own real-world experiences. In order to be effective, though, teachers need to ensure that students are reading interesting texts.

Interesting Texts

Students comprehend more when they are interested in the topic, so it makes sense that they are drawn to interesting and informative texts. Beyond selecting books that match students' individual tastes, teachers can generate additional student interest in texts. Most teachers know that students choose two types of books beyond their own interests: books that have cool covers and books that are introduced by teachers through read-alouds and book talks.

Teachers are salespeople. Both fancy department stores and neighborhood grocery stores boast a variety of visually appealing displays. Stores place the products they want to push the most at the customer's eye level, and those products are designed to capture the buyer's attention. Teachers who want to push certain books need to display them in a way that intrigues students. Taking note of how books are displayed in bookstores, teachers can use similar techniques in organizing the classroom library (Sibberson and Szymusiak 2003, 11–23). Books may be grouped by genre, by author, by topic, or by difficulty levels. Less-familiar titles can be interspersed among popular titles. Series books are favorites of many students, so it's a good idea to place these books together. Sections can be used to highlight new books; to feature "our choices," books that students recommend to one another; and to group books, stories, or articles from read-aloud activities. The goal of such arrangements is to encourage students to engage with a variety of texts, to share their reading interests, and to reread favorites throughout the year. Organizing the classroom library is a task for both teacher and students. Students are likely to have lots of ideas about how to set up the library: they can help with the floor plan, make suggestions for grouping books, create labels for the nonfiction section, and contribute to decisions about how often book displays should be changed.

Teachers are integral in drawing students' attention to particular books. They can make any book appealing by the way they read it aloud. Teachers can take great books like *Where the Wild Things Are* (Sendak 1963) and read them in a boring, monotonous way. Teachers can also read aloud the telephone book in a way that gets all students enthusiastic about reading. The teacher's presentation and choice of books are critical in engaging students' interests. Veronica Carrillo, a third-grade teacher in Los Angeles, was particularly fond of science and only read aloud science-oriented books to her students (Brassell 2007). When her students checked out books to take home every night, they almost exclusively checked out the science books that she read aloud, even though their classroom library contained more books of other genres than science books. By allowing students to choose what they want to read, teachers provide students with the incentive of guiding their own learning.

Autonomy Support

Student interest in a topic determines how teachers use it as a basis for their reading and language arts instruction. Good lessons support students in generating their own questions. This Socratic form of learning enhances comprehension by letting students actively participate in their learning of a topic. By creating thematic units that students help design, teachers empower their learners to "comprehend by doing."

Some teachers face the challenge of knowing that their students will be in classrooms the following year with teachers whose approach to instruction may be constrained by mandates to use prescribed materials and/or limited access to a variety of resources. The challenge for these teachers is to find a way to empower students to take charge of their own learning so that they will succeed regardless of such instructional limitations. One way to "arm" students is with various activities that support their reading autonomy.

By using reading logs (Hancock 1992; Tompkins 2004), students can make predictions, ask questions, and clarify any misunderstandings they may have about what they are reading. Any journal can become a reading log, where students can write their reactions and opinions about books they are reading. Students can color green, yellow, or red beside each book entry to easily identify books that they enjoyed (green), books that were average (yellow), and books that they found boring (red). Students can also add word-wall words, diagrams, and other information they find helpful for each book. Many students improve their comprehension by focusing on particular authors and genres in which they can more easily anticipate the formats of the stories. Those observations explain why teachers should explicitly teach students a variety of strategies in order to assist them in comprehending what they read.

Strategy Instruction

Student interest skyrockets when they perceive themselves as competent at activities. Confident readers are more likely to read more, and the more they read, the better readers they become. To become confident readers who easily comprehend what they read, students need to have comprehension strategies. Teachers need to teach them these strategies.

Giving students answers is a waste of time and a disservice to students. Students do not need answers. Rather, they need *strategies* they can use to find the answers for themselves. Different students require different comprehension strategies, and teachers need to devote time in their classrooms each day to explicitly teaching students reading comprehension strategies. Specific comprehension strategies are discussed in greater detail in the following chapters. The important thing for teachers to consider is that by differentiating comprehension strategies for their students, they can actively engage more of their students in any text they are reading.

Collaboration Support

One of the characteristics Guthrie and Cox (2001) identified of highly engaging classrooms involved students working with peers to form interest groups in which to read and write about a topic in language arts. By varying group sizes and composition (e.g., partners, small groups, teams, whole class), teachers are better able to support the wide range of learners in their classrooms. Student interest is increased when teachers encourage students to share and discuss what they are learning about a topic with their peers.

A four-year-old child looking up at a tall teacher towering over him or her may feel a bit intimidated no matter how nice that teacher is trying to be. Kids and adults think differently, and students often benefit by working more closely with one another than with the teacher because they are more comfortable. As students work more closely with the teacher, this barrier may dissolve. To best determine students' needs and abilities, however, teachers can observe students reading and writing together. Often, students who burst into tears at the beginning of the school year when teachers try to evaluate their "concepts about print," will participate enthusiastically a few weeks later if they are given opportunities to warm up to their teachers.

Evaluation

When Danny asked his young students to write books for children's hospitals and senior centers, he found that his students worked harder and produced better work. They became more actively engaged in comprehending what they read when they saw the end in mind (i.e., a purpose). By allowing students to work in groups to write about and report together on what they read, teachers can create classrooms where students become excited about comprehension as a way of communicating ideas.

Evaluation does not have to be a painful experience. For students who may have difficulties comprehending what they read, standardized tests are like going to the dentist's office with a cavity. Assessment can be fun and meaningful. By allowing students to develop an array of products to showcase their growth and understanding, teachers can accommodate the diverse abilities present in their classrooms. This matter will be discussed in further detail in Chapter 5 on differentiating instruction.

The seven conditions that Guthrie and Cox (2001) identified build a context for reading that motivates students to become more interested in reading. Interest is the starting point for comprehension. Keep in mind that these conditions are not meant for teachers to facilitate in isolation or over a brief period. Conscientious teachers realize that "there are no shortcuts" (Esquith 2004), as reading comprehension is a process that takes time and patience to develop. Proficient readers accumulate a variety of characteristics over time. The next chapter will examine those qualities.

10 Cool Ways to Engage Students' Interest in Reading

1. **Reading Necklaces**—Go to a handicraft store and purchase a bead kit for about $15. Give each of your students a plastic necklace, and every time they read a book, they earn a bead for their necklace. Students walk around the room proudly showing off their necklaces to one another: "Oh, you are a very wise reader. You have many beads."

2. **Green Light: Go**—Go to a discount store or office-supply store and buy simple circle stickers in green, yellow, and red. Create a wall chart or a notebook for students to keep records of the books they like, ones they think are so-so, and ones they don't like. When students read a book they like, encourage them to place a green sticker beside the book title on the wall chart. If they read a so-so book, they can place a yellow sticker on the chart. If they read a book they do not like, they can identify it with a red sticker on the chart. Once a book has five red stickers, have a class discussion about why the book is unpopular, and encourage students to offer suggestions about how it might be improved. This activity can be used to help students share and defend their reading likes and dislikes.

3. **Campfire Interactive Reads**—Create class stories that require audience participation. For example, if you were to create a story about a cowboy riding a horse under the hot sun, every time you read the word *cowboy*, the kids could shout, "yee-haw!" Every time you say "horse," the kids could whinny, and every time you say "sun," the kids could sing, "Feeling hot, hot, hot!"

4. **Read to a Stuffed Animal**—Let students be the teacher by giving each student a stuffed animal that is a "struggling reader." Students get to teach their stuffed animals how to read better. Any students who want to show off their teaching skills can have their stuffed animal read a story aloud to the class.

5. **Right Writes**—Get students excited about reading by getting them excited about writing. Read aloud a story without showing students the cover or telling them the title. After you read the book, ask students to design a cover and give the book a title. Let the class pick their favorite. Another way to get students interested in reading and writing is to stop reading three pages before a story ends and encourage them to write their own endings. Compare their endings to the author's ending and encourage students to email authors with their own versions.

6. **(Your State) Jones**—You're a good-looking archaeologist who discovers amazing treasures every day. You just do not know what they are. Ask students to describe objects in fun ways and make it a game to see how many different uses they can think of for an object. For example, place a staple remover on your "excavation site" and ask students to make predictions about what it could be. Students may predict it is a device to get knots out of shoelaces, an ear piercer, a pincher, a counting device, and even a staple remover. Then, after students get the concept using a concrete object in your class, choose a picture of an object in a book or other text you are reading and repeat the process. This activity helps students build their vocabularies.

7. **Dueling Banjos**—Recite a poem in a number of different ways (e.g., students echo each line after you say it, students slowly rise as they chorally read each line, students recite the poem from a soft whisper to a shout, students sing the poem like a country-western song, etc.).

8. **Mystery Reader**—Have a special day of the week when a guest comes to your class to read to the students. If you cannot find someone to come read to your class, you can always dress up as different characters.

9. **Musical Chairs Reading**—Play like musical chairs, but when the music stops, have poems and short passages on each chair for students to read.

10. **The Book Fairy**—Danny found that his attendance was lowest on Tuesdays, so to encourage his students to come to class on Tuesdays, he designated that day to be the day of the Book Fairy's visit. He placed a special book on each child's seat. For example, Marisol would find a book about horses on her seat with a sticky note attached that would say something like, "Marisol, here is a book about horses. I know how much you love horses. Enjoy reading it! From, The Book Fairy."

Chapter **3**

What Do Proficient Readers Do?

As her fifth graders read a short passage on the Revolutionary War, Mrs. Paulson walks around the room jotting down notes on a clipboard she carries for informally assessing her students. She notices that Tawanna has already finished and asks her to lead her group's discussion when the class breaks into small groups. Jacob and Reginald talk about how many more British forces there were than American forces, while Yovani shades his eyes and concentrates on the text.

"Need any help, Yovani?" Mrs. Paulson asks, and the boy shakes his head.

"I'm reading it again to see how many people George Washington had in his army," he says.

"Is that important?"

"Uh-huh," Carmen contributes. "The British had a lot more guns and soldiers."

"Like the Orcs invading Helm's Deep in Lord of the Rings:The Two Towers," Stanley shouts.

Mrs. Paulsen smiles and asks Stanley who George Washington reminds him of from The Two Towers.

"Aragorn," he replies. "But he don't (sic) become king. He becomes president."

Mrs. Paulsen writes a few notes on her clipboard and praises Stanley for his creative analogy. She asks the rest of the class if anyone can think of another example of one side having so many advantages, and Roneka shouts, "Like David against Goliath in the Bible."

"Like Boise State beating Oklahoma in football," Damon says, and a group of boys around him nod in agreement.

"Good," Mrs. Paulsen says. *She asks the class to write about a time when they felt the odds were against them and the ways they overcame these obstacles.*

You're the Expert

1. How do you informally assess your students' reading comprehension?

2. Think of the different readers in your class. What are some of the qualities you have observed in your best readers?

3. Based on the qualities you just thought of, think of ways you can enrich your other students' reading comprehension by promoting the habits of good readers. Write down some ways you can promote these habits in your classroom each day.

What are the characteristics of a proficient reader? Proficient readers understand the complexities of language. They automatically integrate prior knowledge and experience into their reading; utilize higher-order thinking skills such as analysis, synthesis, and evaluation; and communicate these ideas (Catron and Wingenbach 1986). In fact, many proficient readers have developed a variety of skills that they automatically employ in order to create meaning when they are reading. While different teachers and researchers emphasize different characteristics of proficient readers, Tovani (2000) says that successful readers of all ages use existing knowledge to make sense of new information; ask questions about the text before, during, and after reading; draw inferences from the text; monitor their comprehension; use "fix-up" strategies when meaning breaks down; determine what is important; and synthesize information to create new thinking. This chapter will look more closely at each of these qualities, highlighting observations of proficient readers.

Proficient Readers Use Existing Knowledge to Make Sense of New Information

The previous chapter discussed how to engage students' reading interests. One of the best ways to engage students with text is to build upon their background knowledge. Proficient readers capitalize on their background knowledge before, during, and after reading in order to take an active role in making connections between themselves and the text, the text and other texts, and the text and the world (Keene and Zimmerman 1997).

Students often comprehend better when they think about things they already know. These can be things that they learned about by watching television shows or movies, or things they read about. They can also be things that they have experienced firsthand in their lives. By taking these prior experiences and relating them to texts, students formulate their own understandings and interpretations of different texts. Teachers help students make these connections by focusing discussion, using questions to prompt deeper thinking, using think-alouds to model strategies, and providing opportunities for students to exchange ideas with each other.

From experiences with students of all ages, many teachers have observed that proficient readers see themselves as readers. Learning to read is like learning to ride a bike: it becomes easier with experience. Experience leads to greater confidence and greater confidence leads to proficiency. Bandura (1989) has shown that students who view themselves as capable of performing tasks are more competent at those tasks, leading to a higher likelihood of academic success.

Proficient readers read more than struggling readers. They read more because they are more confident in their reading than struggling readers. These increased encounters with print lead to improved reading ability. Orientation and motivation to read, in fact, have been shown to be critical factors in one's reading comprehension (Mason, Herman, and Au 1991).

Additionally, proficient readers preview the text and predict what they think will happen based on their prior experiences. Accessing their background knowledge, these students can look at different text structures and say things to themselves like, "I think…" "I'll bet…" "I predict…" "I imagine…" and "I wonder…." These students are so excited to share their insights that they talk about what they read with their teacher and others.

Talking about text is an essential element of effective comprehension instruction. Such talk must be purposeful and relevant to the needs and interests of the students. "Purposeful talk is focused, collaborative talk; a social process that requires children to actively engage with ideas, think out loud together, and work to a co-construction of those ideas" (Nichols 2008, 12). Proficient readers benefit from the support that teachers provide when they capitalize on students' eagerness to talk about what they have read.

Proficient Readers Ask Questions About the Text Before, During, and After Reading

Not only do proficient readers demonstrate a willingness and ability to think about what they read and discuss their thoughts with others, but they also enjoy asking lots of questions and responding to what they have read (Mason, Herman, and Au 1991; Tharp and Gallimore 1989). They ask questions of themselves, the authors, and the texts they read. Questioning what they read, in fact, is essential to their reading process.

Successful readers understand how genre will impact the questions they ask and the strategies they select. By teaching students to move fluidly through various strategies, teachers can help students understand when to select a specific strategy. For example, readers need to understand that fiction and nonfiction require very different strategies. Students need to ask themselves different questions when working with texts of differing genres.

Proficient readers generate two types of questions. They may ask literal questions, such as Who? What? Where? or When? in order to determine critical pieces of information in a story. They may also ask inferential questions like Why? How? or What if? to explore different possibilities in stories. Inferential questions highly influence students' interpretations of a text.

Proficient Readers Draw Inferences from the Text

Authors often express more than is actually directly stated in the text—the way people's intonation greatly influences the meaning behind what they say. Proficient readers need to read between the lines to determine what a text actually means. By examining the context of words and passages, proficient readers take their background knowledge and the facts the author has stated and come up with an explanation or interpretation for what has happened.

Without much conscious effort, good readers fill in the missing pieces of a story that an author does not explicitly state. Strategy instruction makes students aware that they have to think about the story and things that they know in order to fill in the gaps. Proficient readers visualize what they are reading by drawing pictures in their heads based on descriptions in the books they read.

Teaching students to make inferences is perhaps one of the most difficult challenges teachers face, as inferences can be abstract concepts to students of all ages. For example, if a student does not have significant background knowledge of a topic, making inferences based on personal experiences can be daunting. Additionally, students often come up with possible explanations for events they read about, but those inferences are not necessarily accurate. These are legitimate concerns that provide support for the benefits of explicitly teaching inference strategies. Students who know strategies for making inferences are better able to monitor their reading comprehension.

Proficient Readers Monitor Their Comprehension

It is important to teach students to monitor and repair comprehension. Again, there are a variety of ways for students to do this, and teachers should teach all of these strategies explicitly and constantly review them with students.

Teachers can train students to consciously select the best strategies to clarify what they read. Students do this when they track their thinking, notice when they lose focus, stop and go back, identify confusing items in the text, and reread to enhance understanding. Good readers are constantly identifying sentences, phrases, and passages that require further clarification by thinking things to themselves like, "I don't understand the part where…" "This…is not clear" "I can't figure out…" and "This is a tricky word because…." Good readers clarify these ideas by rereading the parts they did not understand, thinking about what they know, discussing the unclear passage with a friend, reading on and looking for clues, and restating the passage in their own words.

Proficient readers understand many word meanings and how to determine unknown word meanings from context. The link between vocabulary and comprehension is strong. When students are proficient readers, they have the ability to identify patterns in language and use semantic cues to figure out what words mean (Mason, Herman, and Au 1991). For example, if they are having difficulties with understanding an unfamiliar word, proficient readers may try to determine the word's meaning by using context clues, by examining the word base, prefix, or suffix, or by consulting an alternative source such as a peer, a dictionary, or the teacher.

For teachers, effective vocabulary instruction involves lots of time spent reading (i.e., seeing words multiple times in meaningful contexts), lots of rich talk and talk about text, plenty of time spent reviewing important words, as well as time spent raising students' word consciousness and instructing students on how to relate new words to known words. Proficient readers already have strategies at their disposal to use when coming across words, phrases, and passages that may appear confusing. If they do not understand something, proficient readers use a number of tools to aid comprehension.

Proficient Readers Use "Fix-Up" Strategies When Meaning Breaks Down

When proficient readers have difficulty understanding something that they have read, they have a bag of tools to help them "fix" their comprehension when something gets broken. They use the tools when they cannot figure out the words, when things do not seem right, or the story does not make sense. Proficient readers also know when to use these tools and can determine which one will do the job.

Mehigan (2005) points out that when students are first learning a strategy, teachers should ask students how they use the new strategy, how well it works, if they plan on using it again, and whether something in the strategy needs to be changed. To be active readers, students must prepare themselves to construct meaning from the texts that they read. Using organizational strategies, they identify the most important details of what they read and relate them to their personal experiences through elaboration. They remember material by rehearsing it and constantly monitor their comprehension of whatever they are reading. Teachers who model strategies provide students the guidance they need to understand the processes, participate in guided practice, and eventually apply the strategies independently.

Proficient Readers Figure Out What Is Most Important in Whatever They Read

To figure out what is most important in a book, chapter, paragraph, or sentence that they read, proficient readers summarize. Students can recall critical information about what they read: "The story takes place…" "First… next… then… finally…" "The main point is…" "A problem occurs when…" "This part was about…" "The most important ideas in this text are…" and "Overall, this was about...." Good summaries include key people/items, places, words, ideas, and concepts.

Research (Marzano 1991) has shown that children who are more familiar with narrative story structures (e.g., plot, characters, setting) achieve higher levels of reading comprehension. Proficient readers understand that while narratives tend to have a strong beginning, middle, and end, expository texts may be organized chronologically, functionally, logically, or in some other fashion. They see the details in texts and can identify main ideas, as well as make inferences (Marzano 1991).

As advanced readers go through a text, they use resources that foster comprehension: engaging with the text before they begin reading; setting purposes; relating ideas in text to their prior experience; constructing images; generating summaries; and monitoring their reading (Pressley 2002). Van Tassel-Baska (1998) determined that current curriculum materials directed toward gifted learners should emphasize process skills such as critical thinking and problem solving. In terms of reading, that means that the most proficient readers are entitled to develop their reading abilities by exploring a wide variety of genres and writing styles. For proficient readers to continue to develop their reading and thinking abilities, they need to be exposed to books with rich characters, dynamic plots, and extensive vocabulary. Howell (1987) suggested that one way to provide advanced readers with a challenge is to encourage them to read good literature that features an extensive range of vocabulary in context.

At Your Fingertips

Despite the basal textbook craze across the country, it has been observed that in very few classrooms were proficient readers motivated to read basal readers. The traditional use of a basal reading series typically focuses too much time and attention on mastering the reading process, particularly phonics, rather than encouraging the more proficient readers in a classroom to interact with good literature (Van Tassel-Baska 1998).

McIntosh (1982) reported that the most proficient readers in classrooms often have preferences for science, history, biography, travel, poetry, and informational texts such as atlases, encyclopedias, and how-to books. These students may be drawn to reference material in their thirst for knowledge or need to understand or solve a problem. Interacting with informational books may also provide an opportunity for proficient readers to develop a deep understanding of a particular topic.

Even though proficient readers have the mental acuity to read books well beyond their age range, they still need guidance in the selection of their reading materials. The age appropriateness of the material must be considered.

Proficient Readers Synthesize Information to Create New Thinking

In plain English, proficient readers make sense out of the messages of the texts they read. They can put the pieces of a story together and understand the themes or big ideas in a story, and they understand that their ideas may change as they read. Good readers may not need extensive training in the reading process and instead may benefit from opportunities to synthesize their reading experiences. Teachers play an important role in sustaining the accomplishments of proficient readers. By providing access to materials that vary by genre, topic, format, and difficulty levels, teachers can help students to expand their reading interests and tastes, to become more informed on a variety of topics, and to achieve even greater success in school.

Reading literary and transactional texts involves students in learning to develop thoughtful interpretations of what they are reading. Students need to approach the task as active makers of meaning. Teachers can encourage students to become active participants in the classroom literary community by tailoring their instructional strategies and methods to the needs of their classes and the individuals in those classes.

Unfortunately, not all students are proficient readers. Typically, classroom teachers work with a diverse range of readers, and many struggling readers require extra attention. The next chapter will examine the characteristics of struggling readers and offer tips on how to work with these students.

Some Observable Habits of Proficient Readers

- use multiple strategies to create meaning in what they read
- may focus on a single strategy for a particular type of text
- enjoy reading a wide variety of materials
- enjoy choosing books on their own
- read often (a lot more than struggling readers)
- read quickly (and understand what they read)
- read to learn new information
- relate what they read to their own lives, others' lives, and other texts
- want to choose books
- express broader vocabularies

Chapter 4

Identifying Difficulties in Reading Comprehension

Mr. Mitchell isn't sure if Stephanie has a problem with reading. Stephanie is a fourth-grade student who seems to read rather well. When reading grade-level material, she rarely makes a mistake in reading the words. Moreover, when reading material from her textbooks, she reads at an appropriate rate and her oral reading sounds fluent—good expression and attention to punctuation. When asked to retell what she reads, Stephanie can provide a good summary of the facts and details from her reading.

However, Mr. Mitchell is concerned about Stephanie's comprehension. He notices that although she is able to read well and provide a good summary of facts, she sometimes struggles with stating the main idea of a passage, especially when the main idea is not explicitly stated in the passage itself. He also notes that she seems to have difficulty with answering (and coming up with) questions that are more inferential in nature—questions that require her to make predictions that go beyond the actual facts of the passage. Mr. Mitchell has also recently noticed that Stephanie prefers to read narrative material over informational text and that she seems to gain a better understanding of material when it is presented in story form or chronological order. Informational passages that are organized around higher-order ideas (for example, cause-effect, problem-solution, comparison-contrast) seem to be more difficult for this student.

You're the Expert

Put yourself in Mr. Mitchell's shoes. Is he right to be concerned about Stephanie? Do you agree that she is experiencing difficulty with reading that requires additional instructional attention? If so, how would you characterize Stephanie's reading difficulties? What sort of instruction might you recommend for Stephanie? Do you think that Mr. Mitchell's concerns are unfounded? If so, why do you think this way?

On the surface, identifying students who experience difficulty with reading comprehension and identifying the nature of their reading comprehension problems may seem a rather simple task. Ask a student to read a text. After having him or her read it, ask the student to recall what he or she has read. If the student can provide an adequate retelling of what was read, you can consider that student to be good at comprehending while reading. On the other hand, a limited or incorrect retelling would likely indicate a student whose comprehension processes are not where they should be. This is simple, right? Not quite.

You see, comprehension is something that occurs inside the reader. Teachers cannot actually observe comprehension happening inside a student. Teachers cannot view the brain as the student reads. Even the brain-scan studies that purport to view how readers' brains act while reading give only very limited information about the areas of the brain that are more or less active while reading text.

What teachers can do in assessing reading comprehension and diagnosing difficulties in reading comprehension is, at best, to make indirect inferences that are based largely on a student's response to a text *after* they have read it. When a student provides a retelling of a passage, that passage has already been read. What teachers are observing is the student's meaningful response to the reading.

At Your Fingertips

While reading and providing a retelling or answering questions related to reading can provide some insights into a student's comprehension, there are a number of variables or factors that need to be considered as they may influence how well a student is able to recall what he or she has read. Below are just some of the factors that may impact comprehension. How would you rate each of these factors in regard to how greatly it affects a student's reading comprehension? What other factors might you add to this list?

- **Difficulty of the text**—Does the difficulty or readability of the passage match the actual grade-level placement of the student? Texts written below the student's grade level are more likely to be comprehended, while passages above the student's grade level are more likely to make comprehension more challenging.

- **Type of text**—Is the passage a narrative, expository piece, informational piece, poem, speech, or some other text form? Different text types can be more or less difficult to understand and may require different comprehension processes.

- **The reader's background and interest in a passage**—Does the student already have a lot of background knowledge? If so, he or she is more likely to have a higher level of understanding of the passage. Less background knowledge is likely to result in poorer comprehension. Similarly, if the reader is interested in the topic of the passage, he or she is more likely to understand the passage. Lower levels of interest are more likely to lead to less motivation to read and lower levels of comprehension.

- **Reading comprehension factors**—Is the student able to give a literal retelling of the passage? Can the student reasonably recall and understand the actual facts and details from a passage? Is the reader able to go beyond the literal and make reasonable inferences from the passage? Can the student make predictions about events that are not explicitly stated in the passage itself? Is the reader able to make reasonable critical judgments about the passage that he or she has read?

- **Reading factors other than comprehension**—Poor understanding of a passage may be due to reading process factors other than comprehension. Problems with decoding words will impair comprehension. Struggling with the meaning of key words, even if they are decoded correctly, will negatively impact comprehension. Fluency problems, (e.g., reading the text in a slow, halting manner without appropriate phrasing and expression) will definitely affect a reader's understanding. Is the passage read orally or silently? Some readers comprehend better under one condition than the other.

- **Factors other than reading**—Many factors beyond reading itself may impact how well a reader understands what he or she reads. What is the student's disposition while reading? Is the student adequately rested or is he or she fatigued? Is the student taking medication and, if so, has he or she taken the medication at the time of the reading comprehension assessment? Is the student wearing any corrective eyewear that has been prescribed? Is the location of the assessment environmentally adequate? Is the temperature appropriate? Is there adequate ventilation? Is the student acquainted with the person giving the assessment? Does the student know the purpose of the assessment?

These are just a few of the many factors that can affect how well a student comprehends what he or she reads. Clearly, the process of assessing reading comprehension and diagnosing problems with reading comprehension is a challenge, to say the least. Nevertheless, it is important to try to identify those students who may be experiencing difficulties with reading, as well as the sources of these problems, so that you can provide effective instruction.

This chapter explores how to better understand students' reading comprehension—especially in identifying those students whose comprehension is not appropriate for their grade placement, as well as the nature or source of the reading comprehension problem. Instruction works best when it is targeted at the needs of the learners. Targeted instruction requires teachers to identify needs and to monitor progress.

Teacher-Directed Assessment of Comprehension

Often, when considering assessment of reading comprehension, teachers think of standardized tests that require students to silently read a series of short passages and answer a set of comprehension questions that follow each passage. While such tests do a reasonable job of identifying students who comprehend well and those who have difficulty with comprehension, they are limited in their ability to provide detailed information about the source or nature of the reading comprehension problem.

It is best to examine a reader's comprehension more directly and precisely through close observation and analysis of student's actual reading. This type of assessment has a number of names—informal reading inventories, formative reading assessment, miscue analysis, to name a few. Perhaps the most accurate name is *teacher-directed comprehension assessment*—one teacher, one student. The student reads texts and responds to the reading. The teacher observes, records data, thoughtfully analyzes the data, makes decisions about the student's reading comprehension, and plans instruction that supports the student's learning needs. This approach to assessment provides a much deeper understanding of each student's comprehension, which will lead to precise instruction that will yield the greatest benefit to each reader.

The Texts to Use

In teacher-directed reading assessment, the student is asked to read one or more texts. Of absolute importance is knowing the difficulty level of the passages the student will be asked to read. Teachers will want to know how well their students perform with material at their respective grade levels, whether they are experiencing difficulty at their grade level, and the level at which they read most comfortably.

In order to do this, teachers need to be able to determine the difficulty of the passages they are going to ask their students to read. This is determining the readability of the passages. Readability is most often determined by measuring the difficulty of individual words in a passage and measuring the difficulty of sentences in a passage. There are many formulas that teachers can use to determine the readability of a passage; however, in our age of the Internet, there are websites that provide this service.

One of our favorite resources is found at the Internet Application for Creating Curriculum-Based Assessment Reading Probes website: http://www.interventioncentral.org/htmdocs/tools/okapi/okapi.php

The process is easy to follow and readability results are returned in a timely way. Simply find a passage (up to a maximum of 180 words) that is at an appropriate grade level for students (choose something from a textbook, reading anthology, or leveled series) and type it into the text box at the website above. Click "Create CBA Reading Probes," and the readability generator will calculate the readability in terms of grade level for the passage. We recommend that you try to find at least three passages written at the student's grade level so that you can use them for different assessment tasks—oral reading, silent reading, and listening.

Comprehension Assessment—Preparation

Once teachers find the appropriate passage or passages, the procedure for assessing comprehension is quite simple. Ask the student to read the passage. Follow up the reading by having the student retell the passage and/or have the student respond to a series of questions that you have prepared to test the student's understanding of the text. The questions should include items that reflect the student's literal recall of the passage, the student's inferential meaning of the passage, and finally, the student's critical analysis of the passage. Normally, 10 questions per passage are sufficient to measure comprehension.

Teachers who intend to have students give a retelling of the passage need to have a scoring rubric to guide them in rating the level of the student's comprehension. On the following page is a six-point rubric that allows teachers to judge the quality of their students' retellings (see figure 4.1).

Figure 4.1: Comprehension Rubric

1	No recall or minimal recall of only a fact or two from the passage.
2	Student recalls a number of unrelated facts of varied importance.
3	Student recalls the main idea of the passage with a few supporting details.
4	Student recalls the main idea along with a fairly robust set of supporting details, although not necessarily organized logically or sequentially as presented in the passage.
5	Student recalls a comprehensive summary of the passage, presents it in a logical order and/or with a robust set of details, and includes a main idea statement.
6	Student recalls a comprehensive summary of the passage, presents it in a logical order and/or with a robust set of details, and includes a main idea statement. Student also makes reasonable connections beyond the text to his or her own personal life, another text, etc.

Comprehension Assessment—Procedures

As noted before, it is best to present the student with three passages: one passage for the student to read orally, one passage for him or her to read silently, and one passage to read to the student. The procedures for administering the assessments are simple and straightforward.

Oral Reading

Step 1: Present the student with the passage. Ask the student to read it aloud in his or her best voice. Tell the student that you will be asking some questions about the passage or asking for a retelling of the passage at the end of the reading.

Step 2: As the student reads the passage, mark any uncorrected word-recognition errors while reading. Note the student's rate of reading, use of intonation, and attention to phrasing.

Step 3: At the end of the reading, remove the passage from the view of the student. For aided recall, ask the student the 10 questions you developed about the passage. Score one point for each response.

For unaided recall, ask the student to retell all he or she can remember about the passage. Listen to the student's retelling carefully and focus on the student's ability to capture the main idea and supporting details, as well as his or her ability to go beyond the text itself. Refer to Figure 4.1: Comprehension Rubric for scoring the student's retelling using a six-point rubric (page 53).

With both types of recall tasks, take note of how the student's vocabulary compares to that of the passage that has been read. Suggestions for analyzing the student's responses are provided in the next section of this chapter.

Silent Reading

Step 1: Present the student with the passage. Ask the student to read it silently. Explain that he or she will be answering some questions about the passage or will be retelling the passage at the end of the reading.

Step 2: Observe the student's silent reading behaviors; for example, finger pointing, vocalizing, pauses, facial expressions or gestures, and evidence of rereading.

Step 3: Follow procedures described for the oral reading task.

Listening Comprehension

Step 1: Present the student with the passage. Tell the student that you will read the passage while he or she follows along silently. Tell the student that you will be asking some questions about the passage or will be asking for a retelling of the passage at the end of the reading.

Step 2: As best you can, take note of the student's behavior while you are reading the selection. In particular, observe the student's attentiveness and apparent ability to follow along in the text as you read aloud.

Step 3: Follow procedures described for the oral reading task.

Analysis of Student Reading

Rate the student's comprehension for each of the three tasks. If questions were used to assess comprehension, rate the student's comprehension using the following scale:

90–100%	outstanding comprehension for grade level
70–89%	adequate comprehension for grade level
0–69%	poor comprehension for grade level

A student who consistently scores in the adequate to outstanding range should not be considered at risk for comprehension. Continued reading and meaningful response to texts should occur.

Retelling scores can also point to problems with comprehension. As teachers listen closely to the student's retelling, they should pay attention to the quality of the retelling. Is the student able to go beyond the facts of the passage? Can he or she provide a decent summary that also includes a statement of the main idea? Is he or she able to provide a summary that includes information from other sources, such as the student's own experiences or information gathered from the student's other readings? Rate the student's retelling using the comprehension rubric shown in Figure 4.1 on page 53. The scores can be interpreted in the following way:

5–6	outstanding comprehension for grade level
3–4	adequate comprehension for grade level
1–2	poor comprehension for grade level

Scores consistently in the poor range indicate that the student does not adequately comprehend what he or she reads. At this point, teachers need to determine the source of the comprehension problem.

Word Recognition as a Source of Comprehension Difficulty

For students whose comprehension falls short of grade-level expectations, teachers need to determine the source of the difficulty so that they may provide instructional intervention to address the problem. A student may not be comprehending sufficiently if he or she is not able to adequately decode the words. To determine if this may be the concern for the student, calculate the percentage of words read correctly on the passage read orally. Do this by dividing the number of words read correctly by the total number of words read. If the student is unable to read 90 percent or more of the words correctly, then teachers can assume that word recognition is a concern and a cause of comprehension difficulty (Rasinski 2003). This student needs additional instruction in decoding words accurately.

Fluency as a Source of Comprehension Difficulty

Lack of fluency may also cause comprehension difficulty. To determine if this may be the case, judge the quality of the student's reading.

- Is his or her reading excessively slow compared with what you consider normal for his or her grade level?
- Does his or her oral reading lack the appropriate expression, attention to punctuation, and enthusiasm that you would consider normal for his or her grade level?

If the answer to these questions is yes, then fluency may be a cause of reading comprehension difficulty. Additional instruction in reading fluency may be called for.

Vocabulary and Comprehension Concerns as Sources of Comprehension Problems

If students appear to have no difficulty with word recognition or reading fluency, but still have difficulties with comprehension, you can assume that vocabulary and comprehension concerns are themselves the major causes of the comprehension problems. This is particularly true if the student performs poorly in comprehension when the passage is read to him or her. During this listening comprehension portion of the assessment, the student does not have to deal with word recognition or fluency during the reading. The fact that you are doing the reading for the student means that you are carrying the load for word recognition and fluency. Poor performance on the comprehension questions or the retelling during listening comprehension definitely signals that the student's comprehension problems go beyond problems with decoding and fluency.

Teachers may wish to take an even deeper look at each student's comprehension in order to tease out specific areas of concern. From the aided recall questions, check on students' performance on vocabulary questions, literal comprehension questions, and inferential questions. Poor performance in any one particular area indicates where students may need particularly focused instruction.

From the retelling, determine if the student is able to recall a robust set of details from the passage. If not, the student needs work in identifying important details from what he or she reads. Is the student able to retell the story in a reasonable and logical sequence? If not, the skill of sequencing ideas from reading may need work. Can the student identify the main idea of the passage? If not, main idea comprehension is definitely an area for instruction. Is the student able to generate reasonable inferences or predictions about the information in the passage? Difficulty here indicates that work on inferential comprehension, or making meaning beyond mere recall of facts, is called for.

For students whose comprehension is poor even when their word decoding and fluency are strong, and for students with poor comprehension of a passage that is read to them, the instructional strategies described in this book are essential. The responses of such students provide evidence that they are not sufficiently engaged in making meaning as they read. The instructional activities described in the next chapters are specifically designed to actively involve students in constructing meaning from the text—meaning of the text itself and meaning that goes beyond the boundaries of the text.

All students require instruction and practice in comprehending texts that they read. The strategies presented here are important for all students, regardless of age or level of reading proficiency. However, the ability to identify those students who struggle with comprehension enables teachers to provide them with texts that meet their instructional reading levels and to differentiate instruction so that students who have particular needs and concerns can be provided with instruction that meets those needs.

Tools for Measuring Word-Recognition Accuracy, Automaticity, and Prosody in Oral Reading

In addition to assessing comprehension, students' oral reading can also be used to measure other important aspects of reading: word-recognition accuracy, word-recognition automaticity (a component of fluency), and oral-reading prosody or expression (also a component of fluency). Poor performance in any of these areas may be contributing to poor reading comprehension.

Word-recognition accuracy is assessed by the percentage of words read accurately by students. This is determined by dividing the number of words read accurately by the total number of words in a passage (an alternative approach is to divide the number of uncorrected word-recognition errors by the total number of words in a passage and subtracting from 100). Compare each student's performance against the following norms:

99–100%   outstanding word recognition

92–98%   adequate word recognition

91% and Below poor word recognition

Automaticity in word recognition is determined by calculating the student's reading rate, defined as the number of words read correctly in the first minute of reading of a grade-level passage. Compare each student's performance against these norms for grade level and time of year.

Figure 4.2: Target Reading Rates by Grade Level (in words correct per minute)

Grade	Fall	Winter	Spring
1	0–10 wcpm	10–50 wcpm	30–90 wcpm
2	20–80	40–100	60–130
3	60–110	70–120	80–140
4	70–120	80–130	90–140
5	80–130	90–140	100–150
6	90–140	100–150	110–160
7	100–150	110–160	120–170
8	110–160	120–180	130–180

(Adapted from Rasinski and Padak 2005)

Scores near the bottom or below the ranges indicated in the table suggest that the student may not be sufficiently automatic in his or her word recognition.

Prosody is another component of reading fluency and refers to the reader's ability to read with appropriate and meaningful oral expression while reading a grade-level passage. Prosody may be assessed by rating each student's oral reading with the scale on the following page. Score 1–4 points in each of the four dimensions (see figure 4.3 on pages 60–61). Total scores will range from 4–16 points. Total scores of 8 or below suggest that the student may not be reading with appropriate expression.

Use the following scales to rate reader fluency on the dimensions of expression and volume, phrasing, smoothness, and pace.

Figure 4.3: Multidimensional Reading Prosody Scale

A. Expression and Volume	
1	Reads with little expression or enthusiasm in his or her voice. Reads words as if simply to get them out. Little sense of trying to make text sound like natural language. Tends to read in a quiet voice.
2	Some expression is used. Begins to use voice to make text sound like natural language in some areas of the text, but not others. Focus remains largely on saying the words. Still reads in a quiet voice.
3	Sounds like natural language throughout the better part of the passage. Occasionally slips into expressionless reading. Voice volume is generally appropriate throughout the text.
4	Reads with good expression and enthusiasm throughout the text. Sounds like natural language. Reader is able to vary expression and volume to match his or her interpretation of the passage.

B. Phrasing	
1	monotonic with little sense of phrase boundaries; frequent word-by-word reading
2	frequent two- and three-word phrases, giving the impression of choppy reading; improper stress and intonation that fails to mark ends of sentences and causes
3	mixture of run-ons, midsentence pauses for breath, and possibly some choppiness; reasonable stress/intonation
4	generally well phrased, mostly in clause and sentence units, with adequate attention to expression

C. Smoothness	
1	frequent extended pauses, hesitations, false starts, sound-outs, repetitions, and/or multiple attempts
2	several "rough spots" in text where extended pauses, hesitations, etc., are more frequent and disruptive
3	occasional breaks in smoothness caused by difficulties with specific words and/or structures
4	generally smooth reading with some breaks, but word and structure difficulties are resolved quickly, usually through self-correction

D. Pace (during sections of minimal disruption)	
1	slow and laborious
2	moderately slow
3	uneven mixture of fast and slow reading
4	consistently conversational

(Adapted from Zutell and Rasinski 1991)

Chapter 5

How to Differentiate Instruction for Student Comprehension

Llesenia arrives to the classroom nearly an hour before the first bell rings. She has completed all of her homework perfectly, organized her desk in preparation for the day's lessons, and helps herself to different learning center activities to occupy herself while she awaits the start of school.

José shows up 10 minutes late to class every day. He never has a pencil, and he does not seem to have the ability to sit in his seat for longer than eight minutes.

Anthony completes math exercises well ahead of his classmates, but he struggles during reading time and usually acts up.

Welcome to Ms. Kwon's fourth-grade classroom. It could be just about any classroom in America. One of the epiphanies teachers reach within their first week of teaching is how, no matter what, every classroom is filled with students of mixed abilities and interests. Every student is different. This is the challenge all teachers face: how to differentiate instruction to meet the needs of every student.

In aiding students' comprehension, teachers can create classrooms that meet state and federal standards and maintain high student expectations by supporting all students' learning modalities and differentiating through content, activities (i.e., process), and product, based on students' readiness, interests, profiles of learning, and environments. That can be a lot to remember. A simple mnemonic trick can help teachers always keep differentiation in mind: each student is RIPE for learning when the teacher uses his or her thinking CAP. RIPE stands for readiness, interests, profiles of learning, and environments; CAP stands for content, activities (i.e., process), and product.

At Your Fingertips

It is often difficult for teachers to understand why students cannot comprehend basic concepts. Teachers need to realize that anything is simple . . . once you understand how to do it. What may be simple to one person may be very difficult to another. To demonstrate this point, try the following two games with students or with your colleagues.

Tap and Listen

Get two students and designate one student a "tapper" and the other student a "listener." Give the tapper a song to tap the beat to on a desk (e.g., "America the Beautiful," "Three Blind Mice," "Twinkle, Twinkle Little Star," etc.). Do not tell the listener what the song is. The object of the game is to see if the listener can guess the song that the tapper taps. Most of the time the listener cannot accurately guess the song. The tapper clearly has a song in his or her head, but the taps wind up sounding a lot like random Morse code messages to the listener.

One Up/One Down

Ask for three to four students to come to the front of the classroom. Tell the volunteers that there are only two rules to this game. The first rule is that when it is each student's turn, he or she must say one of three things: "two up," "two down," or "one up and one down." The second rule is that you must alternate your statement on each turn (e.g., if you said "two down" on your last turn, you must say "two up" or "one up and one down" on the next turn). Begin by keeping your arms hanging beside you and saying "two down." Each student must then make a statement, and you will tell each student whether he or she is right or wrong. After everyone takes a turn, rearrange the order of the students and play a few more rounds. Then allow the student volunteers to leave the room while you explain the game to the rest of the class. Ask the remaining students whether they figured out what the game is about (i.e., your statement depends on where your arms are, e.g., if both of your arms are above your head, you say "two up," and if one is in the air and the other is by your waist, you say "one up and one down").

Both games are meant for teachers as well as students. Each game demonstrates the same point: what may seem basic to one person may appear much more complex to another, and it requires patience to determine how to get a point across in a manner that everyone understands.

How can teachers use students' strengths, interests, and background experiences to facilitate instruction? What role does classroom environment play in comprehension? How can teachers vary assignments and assessment strategies to meet the needs of all students? Do you routinely accommodate all students in your class? The rest of this chapter will offer suggestions that can be used in classrooms.

Readiness

Allow students to "show what they know" in different ways. Do you think Joe Montana would be more successful taking a written exam on how to win a Super Bowl, or would he do better if you just gave him the ball with two minutes left to play in the Big Game? Some students will do better if teachers just "give them the ball."

Provide students with plenty of time to explore, understand, and transfer learning to their long-term memories. Permit students time to revisit ideas and concepts in order to connect or extend them. Repetition is not necessarily a bad thing. Any parent of a young child will admit that his or her child always wants to read the same book every night before bedtime. The reason is the child may be memorizing the book. Generally, the child also feels comfortable and familiar with the characters and form of the story. Everybody needs to feel like an expert at something, so allow children opportunities to become "experts" and exhibit "specialties."

Ensure that lessons are developmentally appropriate, tier activities to provide an appropriate level of challenge, and compact curriculum to provide enrichment and challenge. An effective classroom can be organized like a good high school athletics program, which usually has a varsity team, a junior varsity team, and a freshman team. Not all students are ready yet to perform at the most advanced level, but that does not mean they should be denied the opportunity to practice and perform. Success among peers in reading leads to greater success. More importantly, once students perceive themselves as good readers, they read more. And the more they read, the better readers they become. To get them to read more, though, teachers need to offer plenty of materials and activities that match their students' interests.

Interests

Incorporate creativity and offer novel, unique, and engaging activities to capture and sustain students' attention. When one teacher's first graders used to get bored, he would tell them that "Australian Pete" was going to read to the class. He'd then leave the room and return with a heavy accent, saying, "G'day, mates! I just got done puttin' another shrimp on the barbie, and your teacher said you want me to read to you." The kids would cheer and yell, "Yeah, Australian Pete!" This teacher had changed nothing but his accent, but he captured his students' attention in a novel way and sustained their attention during his read-aloud.

By providing students with real choices in what they learn, how they learn, and how they demonstrate their learning (i.e., flexible and varied), teachers can enhance their students' reading comprehension skills. Teachers can teach to standards without sacrificing student interest. Select the standard that needs to be taught and brainstorm a variety of ways in which students can practice learning that standard and show off what they have learned. The more decisions students are allowed to make in the classroom, the more they participate and pay attention. Offer real-world challenges that are directly connected to their lives and students will learn more.

Finally, use multimedia and technology. Computers are popular learning tools for students. What a wonderful resource for teaching students comprehension skills! Many students who are supposedly illiterate can surf the Internet, write emails, and send text messages to their friends on cell phones. These students are not illiterate. They are disinterested in school. Teachers can use the computer to capture their attention. There are countless online tools and software that can enhance students' comprehension while maintaining their interest. Most teachers accept that they must be patient enough to watch their students closely in order to determine how they learn best.

Profile of Learning

Focus on students' learning styles. Gardner (1993) determined that students exhibit multiple intelligences. Instruction should begin where students are academically, and not in the front of the curriculum guide or with the state standards document. Such acknowledgement reveals that teachers are aware of students' needs and interests and draw upon this information to plan instruction. Sternberg (1998) showed that students' minds work in different ways and identified three general types of students in all classrooms: book-smart kids, street-smart kids, and creative thinkers. All of these students need to be and can be taught differently. Some students need opportunities to be physically active rather than constantly sitting still in their desks. By permitting positive movement in the classroom, teachers acknowledge that some students learn better on their toes.

When teachers emphasize student strengths and develop ways to compensate for weaknesses so they do not inhibit what students can do, their students prosper. One way of doing this is for teachers to explicitly instruct their students in reading comprehension strategies. By recognizing and honoring cultural diversity, teachers also demonstrate to students that there is nothing wrong with being different. In fact, all students can learn from the differences around them. In one of Danny's classes, African American students learned to read better because the Latino students shared the strategies they had learned in Spanish. By creating inclusive environments, teachers can encourage their students to take chances.

Environment

Differentiating the environment means building a setting that honors and sustains respectful behaviors (e.g., teacher to students, students to students). By developing a sense of community and creating an environment where students feel comfortable taking risks, teachers can promote the development of a broad range of reading skills and interests. They can do this by organizing the physical space in the classroom to accommodate student-centered activities that incorporate all the senses. For example, Danny's passion is classroom libraries, and his goal has always been aimed at getting students so excited to read in that space that they did not want to do anything else. He did this by allowing students to read anywhere (he had plenty of cushions, carpeting, tents, inflatable rafts, and other cool places to read), with anyone (as long as they were reading), and anything (his library boasted a variety of books of different levels and genres, e.g., magazines, comics, newspapers, menus, encyclopedias, brochures, and so on). His students listened to soft music as they read, and they could eat and drink while they read.

You're the Expert

1. How do you assess your students' reading comprehension? How do you use these assessments to guide your instruction?

2. Think of any lesson you teach. On a sheet of paper, list all the ways you differentiate the lesson to meet the needs of the diverse learners in your class. Keep in mind that "each student is RIPE for learning when the teacher uses his or her thinking CAP."

3. Think of one student who may be struggling in your classroom. Develop a curriculum that can meet his or her specific reading comprehension needs. Keep in mind that good classrooms are designed around the individual needs of students, and this process becomes easier with experience.

4. Review several of your lessons to take an inventory of the various ways in which you differentiate instruction for **R**eadiness,

Interests, **P**rofiles of Learning, and **E**nvironment (RIPE). What does this inventory reveal about your instruction? What are the strengths? What changes would you like to make? How will you go about making these changes?

Content

Providing students with purposeful materials and resources helps capture their interests and sustains their motivation to learn. In these situations, students soon recognize that the teacher has high expectations for them and is confident that they are capable of fulfilling those expectations. To get students started on this track, teachers need to make the content comprehensible to students.

Teachers prefer to have a number of resources they can use to differentiate content for their students. They can present the curriculum through interdisciplinary "big ideas" rather than disconnected small facts. Sometimes it helps to think of curriculum like a jigsaw puzzle. By planning before, during, and after instruction, teachers "think through" all the potential pitfalls that students may encounter in their reading. Such planning creates the big picture, something that usually helps students "get it." No matter how careful teachers are in their planning, though, they always have to be prepared for the unexpected. Teachers know they must constantly adjust the curriculum to match the needs of various students.

Here are just a few ideas for how teachers can differentiate content in reading:

- reading partners/reading buddies
- choral reading/antiphonal reading
- flip books; split journals (e.g., double entry, triple entry)
- books on tape
- highlights on tape
- digests/book summaries

- note-taking organizers

- varied texts

- varied supplementary materials

- highlighted texts

- think-pair-share/preview-midview-postview

Teachers should challenge their students. Vygotsky (1978) came up with the concept of the zone of proximal development (ZPD)—the zone between a student's actual development and his or her level of potential development, or the place where real learning occurs. Basically, Vygotsky theorized that students learn best in settings where adult guidance is available or opportunities are provided for collaboration with more capable peers. Our interpretation of this concept is that students learn best when they are around people who are a little smarter than they are.

Rubrics are excellent guides for students. When teachers clearly state expectations (and are specific about requirements), students prosper. Many students fail not because they do not understand a specific topic, but because they fail to understand the teacher's specifications. When students participate in the development of rubrics, they learn which factors are important for successful learning. Teachers who collaborate with their students in creating rubrics for reading comprehension soon begin to see the benefits of these efforts—students demonstrate understanding of strategies, they know how to regulate and monitor their reading, and they approach reading with greater confidence. Negotiating contracts to provide appropriate learning activities for students motivates them to read better because they understand the expectations for their success.

Activities (Process)

Teachers can empower their students by allowing them to help set and enforce norms and develop standards. During the first month of school, teachers need to train their students in how to run the classroom. For the rest of the year, allow students to do just that—

run the classroom. Students comprehend better when they are forced to actively perform daily routines (rather than being allowed to passively nod in agreement that they understand). By creating centers, teachers can encourage students to take a more active part in their learning. Centers, however, are only one means of increasing students' active participation in the classroom.

Teachers need to use active, hands-on learning. To do this, allow students to work collaboratively and independently (i.e., flexible grouping). The more teachers get their students out of their seats and working together, the better. Teachers who have limited foreign language skills and have predominantly English language learners depend on students to help one another as much as possible. Teachers will find that many students' reading comprehension skills will improve by working with peers and asking a lot of questions and sharing personal interpretations of texts.

Differentiate by varying the strategies. Students respond differently to different strategies. What works really well for one student may not help another student at all. Offer students plenty of time for reflection and goal setting to see if their strategies work. Explicit strategy instruction enables students an "easy way out" of tough spots when they are having a difficult time understanding what they read, and students need to understand which strategies work best for them. By teaching students to aim high and scaffolding to help them overcome weaknesses, students can become better readers.

Consider using integrated curriculum, problem-based learning, and service learning. Students perform better when they have an audience, so facilitate activities that students can use to help the classroom, school, or community. By making use of higher-level thinking and questioning strategies, teachers teach for meaning instead of rote. Students can get just as much out of performing a play about a book they read as they can from writing a book report, but the play will probably stick with them a lot longer.

An optimal differentiated classroom promotes students' reading comprehension by balancing teacher-chosen and teacher-directed activities with student-chosen and student-directed activities. Teachers need to monitor student progress constantly and be flexible (with time, space, materials, and groupings). When teachers collaborate with parents, resource specialists, and other community members, students benefit.

Product

Learning assessments don't have to come from tests only. When you differentiate instruction, you consider students' needs. The same can be said for assessing students' mastery of content. A number of resources can be used to reveal the true learning profile of students. Some alternative sources for student data include journal entries, short-answer tests, open-response tests, home learning, notebooks, oral responses, portfolio entries, exhibitions, culminating products, question writing, and problem solving. Teacher data mechanisms include anecdotal records, observation by checklists, skills checklists, class discussions, small-group interactions, teacher-student conferences, assessment stations, exit cards, problem posing, performance tasks, and rubrics.

There are a variety of project ideas that can capture students' interests and adequately demonstrate student learning. Provide opportunities for projects, creativity, problems, and challenges, and always focus on student growth. Initiate student-maintained portfolios and assessments with varied and original products. Support students in creating products for real events and audiences through public displays and performances. Emphasize quality of thought and expression vs. accuracy.

Dare to Differentiate: 50 Terrific Teacher Tools and Ideas

The following is a list of 50 tools and ideas to try to make sure that each student is RIPE for learning using his or her thinking CAP.

Readiness	
1.	Allow students to show what they know in a variety of ways.
2.	Provide students with plenty of time to explore, understand, and transfer learning to long-term memory.
3.	Give students time to revisit ideas and concepts in order to connect or extend them.
4.	Ensure that lessons are developmentally appropriate.
5.	Tier activities to provide an appropriate level of challenge.
6.	Compact the curriculum to provide enrichment and challenge.
Interest	
7.	Incorporate creativity.
8.	Provide students with real choices in what they learn, how they learn, and how they demonstrate learning (i.e., flexible and varied).
9.	Offer real-world challenges that are directly connected to the students' lives.
10.	Offer novel, unique, and engaging activities to capture and sustain students' attention.
11.	Use multimedia and technology.

Profile of Learning	
12.	Focus on students' learning styles.
13.	Emphasize brain-compatible instruction.
14.	Recognize and honor cultural diversity.
15.	Emphasize students' strengths and develop ways to compensate for weaknesses so that the weaknesses do not inhibit what students can do.
16.	Permit positive movement (many students learn better on their toes).
Environment	
17.	Create a supportive environment of respect (teacher to students, students to students).
18.	Develop a sense of community.
19.	Facilitate an environment where students feel comfortable taking risks.
20.	Promote the development of a broad range of skills and interests that incorporate all senses.
21.	Set up the physical classroom for student-centered instruction.
22.	Provide purposeful materials and resources.
23.	Have high expectations for all.
Content	
24.	Present the curriculum through interdisciplinary "big ideas" vs. disconnected small facts.
25.	Plan before, during, and after instruction.
26.	Negotiate contracts to provide appropriate learning activities for students.

27.	Challenge students.
28.	Create centers.
29.	Co-develop standards with students.
30.	Clearly state expectations and be specific about requirements.
31.	Empower learners! Encourage students to help set and enforce norms.

Activities (Process)

32.	Utilize active, hands-on learning.
33.	Allow students to work collaboratively and independently in flexible groups.
34.	Make use of higher-level thinking and questioning strategies.
35.	Offer students plenty of time for reflection and goal setting.
36.	Vary strategies.
37.	Consider integrated curriculum, problem-based learning, and service learning.
38.	Balance teacher-chosen and teacher-directed activities with student-chosen and student-directed activities.
39.	Help students understand the group's shared needs for success: to belong, to trust, the need for the future, etc.
40.	Monitor student progress constantly.
41.	Aim high and scaffold weaknesses.
42.	Teach for meaning, not rote.
43.	Be flexible with time, space, materials, and groupings!
44.	Teach strategies explicitly so students have an "easy way out" of tough spots.
45.	Collaborate with parents, resource specialists, etc. It takes a village!

Product	
46.	Provide opportunities for projects, creativity, problems, and challenges.
47.	Focus on student growth.
48.	Initiate student-maintained portfolios and assessments with varied and original products.
49.	Support students in creating products for real events and audiences through public displays and performances.
50.	Emphasize quality of thought and expression vs. accuracy.

Differentiation Songs & Dances

Danny has written three songs (one with accompanying dance movements) that have been a huge hit with students and teachers alike. Try teaching these songs to emphasize the importance of differentiating instruction.

The Differentiation Diddy

(to the tune of "Do Wah Diddy Diddy," lyrics by Danny Brassell © copyright 2007)

There I was just about to teach my class,

Singin', "Do what I say. I'm the teacher. Yes, indeed."

Then my students looked at me en mass,

Askin', "Do what you say? Are you kiddin'? We can't read."

They looked stressed (looked stressed),

They looked bored (looked bored),

They looked stressed. They looked bored…

They were not a happy hoard.

I had kids of all sizes. They were different, every one,

Singin', "Do you want to teach a standard or me?"

They asked, "Why is school always work and no fun?"

Sing this: "That is not the way that school has to be!"

I said, "Yes!" (said yes)

"You're all right" (all right)

I said, "Yes! You're all right"

Now our future's lookin' bright.

Our class is now happy, and we learn a lot more.

'Cause we each are different, and we learn differently.

When others critique us, we just shut our door.

And we play. And we sing. And we think critically. Yeah!

Teachin' Has Got You!

(to the beat of "Waddlyacha," lyrics by Danny Brassell © copyright 2007)

(While singing, do each of the following hand movements twice: pat legs, clap hands, slide hands horizontally with right hand on top, slide hands horizontally with left hand on top, hit fists vertically with right hand on top, hit fists vertically with left hand on top, shake right thumb over right shoulder like a hitchhiker, shake left thumb over left shoulder like a hitchhiker.)

Teachin' has got you. Teachin' has got you.

What do you do? What do you do?

(Repeat, and do not forget all the hand movements.)

It's the craziest job. There's quite a lot to it.

I don't know how I'm gonna get though it.

I like the job. It's the job I like best.

I love teaching my students at school!

(faster)

The Newspaper Song

(to the tune of "The Facts of Life," lyrics by Danny Brassell © 2006)

You take the good. You take the bad. You take them both, and there you have a newspaper. A newspaper.

There are sections for business reports, entertainment, news, and sports. A newspaper. A newspaper.

It has everything! You can buy the car of your dreams! It has classifieds and movie times, stories showing local crimes.

You…you…you can share it with your friends and learn the facts of life!

Chapter 6

Comprehension Strategies

Each day, Ms. Ramos asks her third-grade students what strategies they use to understand what they read.

"When I read things that I don't understand, I put a sticky note on that part and keep reading until the end," says Jocelyn. "Then I go back and reread the parts that I didn't understand."

"What do you do if you still do not understand what you read?" Ms. Ramos asks.

"I'll ask Laura or Maya if they understood it, and we'll talk about it," Jocelyn replies.

When Ms. Ramos asks the class if they use different strategies for different types of books, Ethan frantically waves his hand to draw the teacher's attention.

"For picture books, I'll go through all the pictures first and predict what I think is gonna happen," Ethan shares. "When we read an information book, I go through and read the headings and words in bold print to try to figure out what is important."

"Does that work for you?" Ms. Ramos asks.

"Uh-huh," Ethan nods. "And for poems, I sometimes look up words in the dictionary that I don't know."

Sylvia boasts that she visualizes every story in her head and tries to relate each story to her own life.

"If I can relate to the characters, it's easier for me to understand," she declares.

After each student shares his or her strategy, Ms. Ramos points to a classroom bulletin board that lists reading comprehension strategies: predict, monitor/clarify, question, summarize, visualize, make use of prior knowledge, and make inferences. Other students shout which category they think each of their classmates' strategies fall under. Finally, Ms. Ramos asks the class which strategy is the best. As if they were on cue, the students respond in unison.

"Whichever strategy works best for you," they recite.

The previous chapters discussed strategies that proficient readers use and how students need differentiated instruction. How do teachers teach different reading comprehension strategies that are appropriate for every student in the class? This chapter will discuss factors teachers need to keep in mind when teaching strategies to students in order to improve their reading comprehension skills, as well as specific activities teachers can model for students when teaching these strategies.

You're the Expert

1. How often do you review reading comprehension strategies with your students? Do you think teaching and reviewing comprehension strategies daily is a good use of instructional time?

2. What types of text structures do you expose your students to in your classroom? Which text structures seem to be most challenging for your students? What resources can you use to help them deal more effectively with these structures?

3. Pick a student in your class and ask that student what comprehension strategies he or she uses. Prompt the student to think about what he or she does before, during, and after reading and if the strategies vary among different texts.

How and Why We Explicitly Teach Comprehension Strategies

So many popular comprehension strategies are identified by abbreviations that the abbreviations themselves can become confusing: QAR, DRTA, SQ3R, etc. These comprehension strategies begin to sound like characters from a George Lucas movie: "C-3P0, meet SQ3R. R2-D2, this is DRTA." Regardless of the name, strategies can prove powerful to students trying to comprehend what they read, and conscientious teachers explicitly teach their students a variety of strategies.

Teaching multiple strategies simultaneously may be particularly powerful (Pearson and Duke 2002, 224–231; National Reading Panel 2000; Pressley 2001). Pearson and Duke (2002) identified five components of teaching comprehension strategies: an explicit description of the strategy and when and how it should be used; teacher and/or student modeling of the strategy in action; collaborative use of the strategy in action; guided practice using the strategy with gradual release of responsibility; and independent use of the strategy.

At Your Fingertips

When people read a text, they use a variety of strategies to comprehend what they read. Teachers can use minilessons effectively when instructing students in comprehension strategies. As the name implies, a minilesson does not take much time, perhaps five to 15 minutes. As the teacher introduces the lesson, he or she explicitly tells students which strategy they are going to learn and how they will use it in their reading. The teacher may ask students to discuss their prior knowledge of a topic in order to get students thinking about the topic. This should take no longer than a few minutes.

The teacher then needs to show students how to use the strategy, usually through a think-aloud, by vocalizing his or her thoughts while using the strategy. For example, if the teacher wants to demonstrate how to question what he or she reads, the teacher would read aloud a piece of text and ask questions aloud about the text. After modeling this activity a few times, the teacher gradually turns the task over to students to model their own think-alouds as they read the text.

As students practice modeling the strategy, the teacher lends support whenever necessary. For example, occasionally the teacher needs to guide students to particular pieces of text that may pose a problem. As students use the strategy, teachers should ask students how well they feel the strategy works. After all, students are not going to continue to use a strategy they aren't confident about. By providing students with time to practice the strategy in front of one another, the teacher ensures that students feel capable of using the strategy on their own.

Finally, students need to practice the strategy on their own. Teachers should provide plenty of opportunities for students to practice a strategy. Additionally, teachers should ask students what they have learned from the strategy and where and how they might use the strategy, for different texts. By getting students to think about how and why they use different strategies (as well as when a strategy may be appropriate), teachers can better support the needs of their students as they try to develop a cache of activities to support each strategy.

In making comprehension instruction explicit, the teacher plays an important role by modeling, explaining, questioning, scaffolding student responses, and gradually releasing responsibility so that students can use the strategies independently.

Using Background Knowledge

Students can make use of their background knowledge (e.g., personal history, interest, experiences, and learning) in order to predict and confirm what they read. They do this by creating text-to-self connections (e.g., memories, emotions, and things that remind readers of common experiences), text-to-text connections (e.g., something previously read, seen, or heard), and text-to-world connections (i.e., reminds reader of world events). Research has demonstrated that children rely heavily on their background knowledge in their interactions with text. McKeown and Beck (2003) have found that leading activities like a Text Talk (i.e., a read-aloud procedure in which teachers ask questions of students throughout the read-aloud) increases students' reliance on the text in both understanding and recalling the text. This occurs when teachers lead targeted prereading discussions and use open-ended questions. Teachers can use a number of techniques to encourage students to relate their background knowledge to what they read: think-alouds (i.e., reader vocalizes thoughts, questions, predictions as he or she reads), sticky notes (i.e., reader places sticky notes in book at points of confusion), Venn diagrams (i.e., student draws two overlapping circles and in the center writes how two items are similar, and writes how each item differs from the other outside the overlap), and graphic organizers like K-W-L+ (i.e., at various points in reading a text, student writes on a chart what he or she already knows, wants to know, has learned, and still wants to learn). Teaching students to draw upon their background knowledge as they read plays a critical role in how effectively they comprehend what they are reading.

Reciprocal Teaching

When students monitor or clarify their reading, they pay attention to points in the text that do not make sense and figure out how to understand these parts. Proficient readers are better at anticipating points in the text that may present difficulties and have fix-up strategies already on hand to deal with such problems. Reciprocal teaching (Oczkus 2003; Palincsar and Brown 1984) is one instructional activity teachers use to engage students in discussion about confusing segments of text with the purpose of gaining meaning from the text and self-monitoring. This instructional approach is designed to focus student attention on four reading comprehension strategies: asking questions, clarifying what was read, summarizing the information, and predicting what might follow. Through this approach, teachers train students to always "stop and think" when they come to a point in a passage that they do not understand. Students are taught to ask themselves if the passage makes sense to them, and if it does not, they should reread the passage, read ahead, look up any confusing words, or ask others for help.

Directed Reading-Thinking Activity (DRTA) is another instructional approach in which the teacher guides students to make predictions about a text, asks them to examine the evidence in the text, and allows them to revise and generate new predictions as they read (Stauffer 1969).

Questioning

Questioning may be one of the simplest yet most powerful ways for students to better comprehend what they read. Questioning helps the reader clarify ideas and deepen understanding. Question answering and question-answering instruction has been shown to lead to an improvement in reading comprehension (McKeown and Beck 2003; Pressley and Forrest-Pressley 1985). Asking a variety of questions is important in order to prompt students to think at all levels of their reading development. For example, Raphael's Question-Answer Relationships (QAR) activity (1984) has been shown to support students in thinking about questions generated by teachers and others. When students ask themselves questions like "I wonder…?" "Why…?" "What if…?" "What does this mean?" and "Does this make sense?" they guide themselves toward a better idea of what they are reading. Teachers offer students a variety of ways to question themselves and others as they read, including think-alouds, sticky notes, question charts (i.e., reader keeps a list of questions/ page numbers), picture walks (i.e., for narrative texts, reader predicts what is going to happen in a story solely by looking at pictures), think questions (i.e., for expository texts, reader examines titles and subheads and asks questions), reciprocal teaching, etc. If students manage to ask themselves good questions, questioning strategies may be the most useful for students in promoting meaning before, during, and after reading.

Visualizing

Sensory images are the pictures, smells, sounds, tastes, and feelings students experience while reading. Students that create images while reading want to continue reading without stopping because they are actively engaged, respond appropriately to the texts they read (e.g., laugh, show surprise, etc.), orally read with expression, make predictions, and elaborate on what they read through discussions with others. Visualization has been shown to be especially useful for students learning about text structure. Baumann and Bergeron (1993) found that when teachers created story maps with their first graders, their students performed significantly better on measures of their ability to identify important story elements. A variety of visualization strategies exist, including think-alouds, drawing pictures (i.e., reader draws pictures of images created in his or her mind while reading), skits (i.e., reader dramatizes story), mind maps (i.e., using a picture of a mind, reader writes and draws thoughts from reading), picture walks, etc. By encouraging students to visualize as they read, teachers provide students with another useful strategy in their quest to comprehend what they read.

Inferring

Drawing inferences is the process of forming best guesses based on the evidence presented in reading passages. It is at the center of students' active construction of meaning when they read (Anderson and Pearson 1984). When students make predictions before or during reading, they are making inferences (i.e., using multiple pieces of information that is found in the text or combining information supplied by the author with students' background knowledge in order to construct meaning). Hansen and Pearson (1983) put together activation of prior knowledge, direct instruction in an inference-making strategy, posing of inferential questions, and predicting to create activities that allowed students to make better inferences. After reading a story and discussing a few important ideas with students, the teacher creates a previous-experience question (e.g., "Have you ever…?") so that students can better predict what they think may happen next. Students read the selection to verify if their predictions are accurate and then discuss how accurate their predictions were. Other activities include think-alouds, using cartoons (i.e., allowing students to write the "thoughts" of characters in bubbles above their heads), 20 Questions (i.e., students ask questions that build on each other so that they can determine a specific piece of information), sticky notes, and similes (i.e., students compare two seemingly unrelated objects). The better students become at making inferences, the better they can identify the most critical pieces of information in a reading selection.

Summarizing

Finally, summarizing is the process of weeding though all of the information and focusing on the main idea. Some researchers have argued that summarization is the most effective comprehension strategy of all (Pressley et al.1989). In determining the importance of what they read, proficient readers understand the purpose of reading different materials, use the text features to assist their understanding, prioritize information, and constantly seek clues in the text. Teachers can model the process of summarizing by providing students with summaries of selections that they have read and encouraging students to use titles, illustrations, topic sentences, headings, and other text clues to determine the importance of what they read. Some of the activities that teachers use to teach summarization include think-alouds; say something (i.e., students stop periodically while reading texts and "say something" about their reading to a partner, e.g., a summary); sticky notes; graphic organizers (e.g., semantic webs that highlight the main idea and supporting details); summary frames (i.e., another graphic organizer that enables students to focus on the most important details of what they read); and discussions of stories.

Instructing students in specific reading comprehension strategies and understanding how to guide students through those strategies are crucial to successful reading teachers. The strategies and activities outlined in this chapter form the basis of strategies that teachers can train students to use before, during, and after reading. The following chapter specifically addresses strategies students can use before reading.

Getting to Know Types of Expository Text Structures

As students advance through the elementary school years, the expectations and requirements for them to read expository texts increase. Narrative material is most commonly used in reading programs, which means that some students may not have had adequate opportunities to learn about the unique features of expository text and how to adapt their strategies to read such text effectively. Furthermore, recent research has revealed that even young children are interested in reading nonfiction and can benefit from instruction based on informational texts (Duke & Bennett-Armistead 2003; Duke 2004). Understanding the structure of expository texts is a good place to start as teachers help their students broaden the application of their reading strategies. Expository text (typically more informational in nature) varies more widely than narrative text (the type of text found in stories). Meyer and Rice (1984) identified the following types of expository text structures:

Definition/List

Definition—This type of structure provides descriptive details about characteristics, actions, etc. This type also includes structures that define concepts and provide examples.

Signal words—*to begin with, for example, most important, for instance*

Graphic organizers—List/Link, lists, webs

Time Order/Chronological

Definition—This type of structure follows a sequence of events in a process.

Signal words—*first, second, then, next, tomorrow, finally, earlier, after,* and *dates*

Graphic organizers—sequence chart, storyboard, layered book, flowchart, time line

Explanation/Process

Definition—This type of structure follows how something works. Following steps in a process is the focus.

Signal words—*first, second, then, next, tomorrow, finally, earlier, after,* and *dates*

Graphic organizers—sequence chart, flowchart

Compare/Contrast

Definition—This type of structure presents similarities and differences.

Signal words—*like, unlike, but, in contrast, however, on the other hand, although, similar, different*

Graphic organizers—Venn diagram, T-chart, three-flap book

Problem/Solution

Definition—This type of structure presents a statement of a problem, question, or remark, followed by a solution, answer, or reply.

Signal words—*so this led to, if…then, problem, solution, one reason*

Graphic organizer—T-chart, flowchart

Cause/Effect

Definition—This type of structure presents an effect along with a reason or explanation (i.e., cause) for that effect.

Signal words—*therefore, thus, because, cause, effect, as a result, since*

Graphic organizers—T-chart, vocabulary strip book

Chapter 7

Comprehension Strategies for Before Reading

Mrs. Olvera's sixth graders have been looking at different fiction books and predicting whether they appear to be realistic or contrived.

"This one looks real," announces Pablo as he holds a copy of Crossing the Wire *(Hobbs 2006) high in the air.*

"What makes you think that?" asks Mrs. Olvera.

"Well, the cover shows a kid in the desert trying to hop a fence," Pablo replies.

"Why does that appear to be realistic to you?"

"'Cause that happens all the time."

Mrs. Olvera nods and looks at the entire class.

"Can anyone think of a time they have seen a boy jump a fence like in the picture on the cover of Pablo's book?" she asks.

More than half of the students in the class raise their hands. Most students are nodding and saying things to the teacher, one another, or anyone who wants to listen. Mrs. Olvera smiles and calls on Vanessa.

"My brothers hop fences when they have to get balls out of people's yards."

"Me, too," Peyton interrupts.

"That is a good example," Mrs. Olvera affirms. "Can anyone think of another time when people may jump over fences? Try and think about

the news article we read yesterday in class." (The class read an article about illegal immigration.)

"Lots of people from Mexico cross the desert in California and Texas to get to America," Pablo says.

"Arizona, too!" shouts Ephraim.

"Do you think this book is about a boy crossing the Mexican American border?" Mrs. Olvera asks.

All the students nod.

"It says so on the back cover," Marco says, and the boys at his table nod in agreement.

Mrs. Olvera asks the entire class to read the back cover. After a minute, she asks the class if they agree with Marco and everyone raises their hands. Mrs. Olvera puts a hand on Marco's shoulder and compliments him for being clever enough to search for clues beyond the book's front cover art.

"What other clues make you think this is a realistic story?" Mrs. Olvera asks.

"The author is Will Hobbs," offers Rasheeda. "The other books we have read by him are about boys doing things that can really happen."

Mrs. Olvera congratulates the class on being able to pick out so many details just from looking at the front and back cover. She tells the class that they are going to spend the next week reading this book, but first she would like students to write on note cards why they think the boy would try to cross a fence between Mexico and America, and then share their ideas with a partner. After about 10 minutes, Mrs. Olvera asks partners to share their predictions with the entire class as she writes each idea on a sheet of chart paper labeled "What we think is going to happen."

Predictions and anticipation provide a critical context for comprehension. Comprehension is an ongoing process. It is not limited to activities during and after reading. How can teachers teach students to think about a text before they read it? How can this assist comprehension of a given text? This chapter will review strategies teachers may use with students to preview a text before they read it, whether it is a piece of fiction or nonfiction.

You're the Expert

1. What do you do to prepare your students to read a new selection?

2. When students have limited background knowledge on a subject, what do you do to make a subject more comprehensible?

3. Find a book on a topic you know nothing about and preread it. Then read it. Think about the strategies you used to help you better comprehend the topic before you read about it.

Prereading exercises are a necessary and motivating step in comprehending a text. Unfortunately, too often, teachers are mandated to follow scripted procedures specified in the district's prescribed instructional series. True, a lot of the activities students are encouraged to engage in before they read a text are old concepts with catchy names. The way to "sell" students on any strategy is to present it with a little pizzazz. Would students rather learn how to "make inferences" or "solve the crime"? Car manufacturers know this. They do not sell cars called "family car" and "midlife-crisis vehicle." They sell Toyota Corollas and Porsche Boxsters.

Teachers can help their students prepare to read by helping them activate what they already know about situations, events, characters, and ideas in the text. Additionally, it is important for teachers to provide students with important background information relevant to the selection (thoughtful teachers constantly question students in a Socratic way to draw out students' knowledge). Students need to learn how to preview a text and make predictions, and it is important for students to be able to identify appropriate strategies for different types of texts. The goal of all prereading exercises is to assist readers in understanding the purpose of what they are reading and using their background knowledge to make predictions about ideas in the text.

At Your Fingertips

Prior to reading, readers should ask themselves a variety of questions. Do I have a clear idea of the topic or purpose of this selection? Have I mentally summarized what I already know about the topic? Have I written down questions I hope to answer by reading this selection? Here are a few tips to consider when previewing a text (please note that many of these strategies work better with informational text than with narratives):

1. Look for books related to whatever you are reading.
2. Look at the front and back covers of the book.
3. Look at the chapter titles.
4. Read the introduction.
5. Read all (if any) subheadings.
6. Read the first and last sentences of each paragraph.
7. Look at graphs, diagrams, and pictures. Read captions.
8. Read the chapter summaries (if any).
9. Read question stems (if any).
10. Determine if the reading is a work of fiction or nonfiction.

Reading begins before a book is opened. Prereading strategies allow students to think about what they already know about a given topic and predict what they will read or hear. Before students read any text, teachers can direct their attention to how a text is organized, teach unfamiliar vocabulary or concepts, search for the main idea, and provide students with a purpose for reading or listening. Most importantly, teachers can use prereading strategies to increase students' interest in a text.

Activating Students' Prior Knowledge

Students bring a vast array of experiences to the classroom. It is the teacher's responsibility to show students how to relate those experiences to any given text. Students need to be able to review a text before they read it and anticipate how it relates to their own experiences. Teachers can model for students questions they can ask themselves before reading a text. For example, in addition to the questions Mrs. Olvera asked her students to think about before reading *Crossing the Wire*, she could have asked other questions such as the following: Why do you think a boy would risk crossing over a wire if he knew he could get into trouble? Is it ever right to break a rule? When have you or someone you know broken a rule in order to do something positive?

You Make the Call

We refer to this activity as "You Make the Call." This is a catchy name for an old-fashioned comprehension exercise. As an anticipation guide, give students a brief reading passage to capture their interest in a topic. The teacher takes short passages from the text itself or texts that describe similar situations (e.g., newspaper and magazine articles). Make sure to choose something that is "catchy" that makes students eager to read the full text (the activity should work in the same way that a movie trailer builds anticipation to see a movie). Read the passage to the students or provide copies for them to read on their own; follow up the reading with a discussion in which students share their ideas about the topic and connections with their experiences (e.g., personal knowledge, other texts they have read, topics they have discussed in other settings). Think-pair-share is another way in which students can respond to their predictions about the material. In think-pair-share, students read a passage, take a few minutes to think about what they have read, then get together with partners and share their observations. To conclude this activity, teachers usually bring the group together to report on the individual partner sharing.

Idea Survey

Provide students with a checklist of statements before they read a passage, and ask them to mark an X beside the statements with which they agree. Three to five statements are usually enough. You can also allow students to look back over this survey after reading the selection to see if their opinions have changed. For example, before reading *Crossing the Wire*, students could mark if they agree with the following statements:

1. Crossing the border from Mexico to America is dangerous.
2. It is all right to quit if you try once and fail.
3. Illegal immigration is always a bad thing.
4. Children are too young to make a difference.

Building Students' Background Knowledge

If a selection deals with a topic that may be unfamiliar to students, the teacher needs to help build students' background knowledge. As students come to classrooms with a vast array of experiences, it is impossible for a teacher to predict each student's background knowledge. It is better to overprepare than to underprepare. Teachers can use DVD and television clips, Internet articles, guest speakers, photos, realia, and other items to help students become familiar with topics being studied. The best resource is usually the students, as some students will have a better knowledge of certain topics than others. Engage these students as "topic specialists" who act as assistants to students who may be struggling with a new topic.

Realia

In reading instruction, realia simply refers to a collection of artifacts that relate to a particular topic. Some teachers call them mini-museums. Realia can be any type of authentic object, including maps, food, music, jewelry, clothing, household appliances, and photographs. When teachers use realia, they have a concrete way to talk with students about a topic for which the students may have limited background knowledge or experience. Teachers can hold up one artifact after another, describe it, and invite students to talk about how the item may fit into a story they have read or will be reading. As students handle one item after another, they are more likely to reveal what they know or don't know about the topic—some students may even bring in artifacts of their own. Antique stores, old volumes from libraries, auctions, garage sales, parents, and grandparents are all potentially wonderful sources of realia materials.

Preview Scavenger Hunts

Encourage students to preview a text to see if they can guess what it may be about. One way students can preview a text is by filling out surveys that act as scavenger hunts. For example, a preview scavenger hunt could survey students to find items in a text like titles, subheadings, pictures, captions, graphics, maps, bold print, italicized words, margin notes, chapter summaries, and chapter questions. After students "hunt" for information, the teacher asks students in pairs, small groups, and ultimately as a class to share any personal connections they may have to the information. The activity should take no longer than 5–10 minutes and usually also acts as a way to get students excited about a particular text. In addition, this activity is effective in helping students become familiar with the format of expository texts.

K-W-L+

K-W-L+ (Brassell and Flood 2004; Ogle 1986) can also be used to activate what students know and need to know before reading. Individually, in small groups, or as a class, have students design a chart with four columns, indicating in the first what they know about a topic; in the second, what they want to know; and in the third, what they learned after they read. A variation could be: What do we know? What do we think we know? What do we need or want to know? The final column (+) is reserved for things that we want to know about a topic that we did not learn from our readings. The focus of K-W-L+ as a before-reading activity rests on what students already know about a topic and what they want to learn.

Determining Purpose for Reading

It is important for teachers to encourage students to use predictions to set a purpose for reading in order to engage them in the reading process. Informational texts have very different formats than narrative texts, and it should be noted that while people read narrative texts primarily for pleasure, they read informational texts for additional reasons, including to learn new concepts and skills. Proficient readers examine the formats of texts before they read in order to help form predictions.

The Vinnie Barbarino Technique

Back in the 1970s, John Travolta played a confused high school student on TV's *Welcome Back, Kotter* who would, whenever he could not answer one of his teacher's questions, always blankly redirect questions back to his teacher. Teachers need to encourage students to use questions as a means of making connections between what they know and what they expect to learn from reading a text. This comprehension activity can be dubbed the "Vinnie Barbarino Technique." Before reading the first section of any chapter, ask students to mentally or in writing turn a chapter heading, subheading, or boldface term into a question, using the 5Ws + H (Who? What? When? Where? Why? How?) Some students will need guidance through this activity several times before they master it because a number of pitfalls can prevent students from understanding a passage. Just think how different the reactions of students will be when asked to use the Vinnie Barbarino Technique instead of SQ3R!

Teachers need to be aware that predictions often run the risk of simply being guesses, with little thought about backing them up. If students look at both the title of a selection and the cover illustration, they are likely to rely primarily on the illustration. It is important, therefore, for teachers to guide the discussion. Oczkus (2003) prompts students to activate prior knowledge by first discussing the title and having students tell what they already know about the given topic.

Nostradamus

Some students have difficulty making predictions for a variety of reasons, including a limited background of experience, failure to activate prior knowledge, difficulty inferring, or reluctance to take a risk. "Nostradamus" is a game that teachers can play with students to encourage them to preread with a keener sense. The teacher asks students to make predictions every day about routine things in their lives (e.g., What do you think is going to be on the lunch menu today? What do you think tomorrow's weather will be? What do you think tomorrow's assembly will be about? How much time will you need to complete your math homework? Which team will win the basketball game?). The name "Nostradamus" itself could be used in an activity to encourage students to make predictions, ones that would have to be verified through some research on the name. (Nostradamus, 1503–1566, was a French philosopher and astrologer whose prophecies about world events are still read and interpreted today.) Check out the History Channel program at http://www.history.com and enter Nostradamus in the search field for more information. By emphasizing to students that predictions are just careful guesses, teachers can encourage students to use predictions to help them better understand what they are reading (and students must not worry about making incorrect predictions, as predictions are simply educated guesses).

When students are in the early stages of implementing a strategy, ask them how they used the strategy, how well the strategy worked, if they would use it again, and whether it needs to be changed (Mehigan 2005). Asking students to constantly think about the strategies that they are using helps students determine the usefulness of any prereading strategy.

Understanding Elements and Structure of Texts

If students are to comprehend what they read, they must first understand the elements and structures of different texts. Additionally, teachers need to provide students with strategies for reading different types of texts. Teachers can accomplish this by devoting less than 15 minutes a day to explicitly teaching minilessons before students read a text.

For example, teachers can explain to students that works of fiction focus on "imagined" people, places, and events. Fictitious narratives stimulate readers' imaginations and communicate the author's perception or view of the world. Fiction includes short stories, legends, myths, and novels. All are made up of the same basic elements: people (characters), places (setting), events (plot), point of view, conflict, and theme. Understanding the structure and elements of a story before reading it can greatly assist students in their comprehension of narrative texts.

Nonfiction works, or informative texts, deal with reality. Essays, articles, editorials, letters, journals, biographies, autobiographies, speeches, and nonfiction books are all examples of informative texts. Students need to understand that informative texts can be organized in ways that are very different from narratives. Students may need to read informative texts more slowly than works of fiction (and sometimes, they may even need to reread informative texts in order to comprehend facts and main ideas). Providing students with instruction about the structure of expository text and practice examining those structures in content-area textbooks as well as other informational resources will enable them to recognize how to adapt their strategies when reading these materials. (See Chapter 6 for information about expository text structures.)

True or False

Some teachers constantly ask their students "true or false" before they read a story. Before reading, students are asked to look at different elements of a story (e.g., pictures, title, headings, cover) and ask themselves if they think that what they are going to read is based on imagined or realistic events. One fourth-grade teacher introduces the concept by giving students tabloid newspapers and magazines, along with regular newspapers and magazines, and asking students to determine which sources provide more reliable information.

Working with Words

Vocabulary knowledge plays an important role in students' reading comprehension. Put simply, if students do not understand many of the words used in a text, they are not likely to understand the text. Although research has shown that vocabulary knowledge plays a critical role in students' literacy development, many teachers devote very little class time to vocabulary instruction (Scott, Jamieson-Noel, and Asselin 2003). Moreover, teachers who do devote time to vocabulary instruction often use strategies that fail to increase students' vocabularies and comprehension abilities (see reviews in Blachowicz and Fisher 2002; Nagy 1988).

Memorizing vocabulary for a test or studying lists of words isolated from the reading experience have virtually no effect on improving one's vocabulary or comprehension (Nelson-Herber 1986). Teachers who provide vocabulary-building strategies that develop concepts beyond straight definitions give their students a better understanding of how words may be used to apply to their own lives. Therefore, target vocabulary words selected for the purpose of prereading should be selected judiciously, and a variety of instructional techniques should be employed. Three criteria to keep in mind when selecting words for study include the relation of a word to key concepts in the text, the students' background, and the potential for enhancing independent learning.

In addition, how much a teacher decides to focus on target vocabulary words before reading depends on his or her approach to a selection. For example, if the teacher reads a text aloud to students, an oral interpretation may convey the meanings of the unfamiliar words. Effective vocabulary instruction before reading a text emphasizes useful words (e.g., sight words/high-frequency words), important words (i.e., words that are integral to the overall understanding of a text), and difficult words (e.g., words that may have multiple meanings, depending on the context). Vocabulary should be emphasized as a means to comprehension through a number of games and other useful strategies, some of which are described in the following sections.

Lex I Con

Introduce five to seven target vocabulary words and ask students to brainstorm the words' meanings in small groups. Often, students with various backgrounds can deduce what new words mean based on their prior experiences. This is also known as a "vocabulary self-collection strategy." For example, when a teacher introduces the term canine to a class of first graders, one little boy might say it means *dog* because the police who drove around his block with a dog in the car had *K–9* written on the side of the squad car.

Prevoke

Prevoke stands for "prediction based on vocabulary." It is a method for getting students to anticipate or predict the meaning of a passage from a set of words provided by the teacher. Prevoke can easily be an extension of the Lex I Con strategy mentioned above. Teachers choose a set of key words from a selection to be read. Students are introduced to the words and their meanings. Students are asked to read the words and categorize them according to the elements of story: words referring to characters, setting, story problems, and story resolution. Students may also be asked to create and justify their own categories for sorting the words.

Once the words are sorted, students are then asked to use the words, as well as the way they sorted the words, to predict what the story will be about. The process of predicting or constructing a hypothetical meaning for a text is comprehension, or making meaning. Even though it is likely that students will not be able to predict the actual story told by the author, the process of actively involving oneself in making meaning is the key to successful comprehension. Too many readers who struggle with comprehension may be characterized as passive readers who do not normally engage themselves in the process of making meaning. Prevoke is a great antidote for those students who are passive readers.

Multiplex

Teachers need to emphasize that the best way for students to understand words is to see those words used in multiple contexts. The best way to do that is through independent reading. Teachers can make sentence strips out of sentences from different stories that use the same word in different ways. Students discuss how a word meant different things based on how the word was used. In this way, students also observe how to use context as a way to figure out what a word means.

Silly Talk

Students greatly expand their vocabularies when they understand that relatively few prefixes and suffixes are used to create words. Teachers can use a "morphemic analysis" (Manzo and Manzo 1990) activity where students create silly words using their knowledge of word parts (bases, prefixes, or suffixes). For example, students would better comprehend words with prefixes like *pro* and *anti* that appear in passages after creating their own silly words that demonstrate that *pro* means "in favor of" and *anti* means "against." Second graders would share that they were "pro-recess" and "pro-pizza party," as well as "anti-homework" and "anti-time-out."

Other useful prereading vocabulary strategies include analogies, interactive word walls, word plays, and idioms (Brassell and Flood 2004). As Stahl (1986) argues, teachers should keep in mind the following three guidelines for effective vocabulary instruction: give both context and definitions for words, encourage students to make new words part of their working vocabularies, and give students multiple exposures to words in a variety of contexts.

Providing students with prereading opportunities can be critical to students' comprehension of a text. This chapter has examined some techniques that are useful in getting students to think about a text before they read it. The following chapter specifically addresses strategies students can use as they read a text.

Some General Tips Before Reading

1. Set a purpose for reading.

   a. Are you reading to get a broad overview?

   b. Are you reading for details?

   c. Are you trying to answer specific questions or prepare for a test?

2. Review all questions at the end. What kinds of questions are you trying to answer?

   a. literal—stated in black and white

   b. critical—read between the lines

   c. applied—on your own

3. Review all maps, graphs, and charts.

4. Acquaint yourself with all new or technical vocabulary.

5. Be sure your surroundings are conducive to reading.

Chapter 8

Comprehension Strategies for During Reading

Mrs. Wynelda reads aloud the big book version of Jon Scieszka's The Stinky Cheese Man and Other Fairly Stupid Tales *(1992) to her first graders. The book is filled with quirky takes on traditional tales like "The Ugly Duckling." Scieszka's version is called "The Really Ugly Duckling," and Mrs. Wynelda's students immediately laugh when they hear the title and see illustrator Lane Smith's silly duckling picture.*

"Why are you laughing?" Mrs. Wynelda asks.

Jermaine laughs and points at the picture of the really ugly duckling. Diego says that the title of the story is funny.

As Mrs. Wynelda reads the story, she stops and asks the class if the story sounds like another story that they have read.

"Uh-huh," Jeanette nods. "It's just like 'The Ugly Duckling.'"

Mrs. Wynelda asks the class if they agree, and all students raise their hands. The teacher tells the class that the stories sound very similar, and she keeps asking herself why this story is called "The Really Ugly Duckling." Jermaine points to the picture again, and Mrs. Wynelda agrees that this certainly is a really ugly duckling. She wonders aloud if the story is going to be any different than "The Ugly Duckling," and several students shrug while a few others nod their heads.

When Mrs. Wynelda turns the page, students giggle to see a grown-up picture of the duckling. The duckling looks the same, just bigger. Mrs. Wynelda asks the class if they see any difference in the story, and DeShon thrusts his arm in the air.

"The duck stays ugly," he erupts. "He doesn't become a swan!"

Classmates nod, and Mrs. Wynelda laughs as she reads that the really ugly duckling grew up to be just a really ugly duck.

Teachers may use a variety of approaches to expose students to a text for the first time. Sometimes teachers ask students to read a passage on their own silently, while occasionally, teachers ask students to read together in pairs or small groups. Many teachers prefer to introduce new topics and texts to students—regardless of their ages—through teacher read-alouds. As the teacher reads, he or she can demonstrate a number of strategies that students may use independently as they read. During reading, students learn to make sense of a text and construct meaning by thinking about the ideas in the passage, connecting these to their prereading predictions, and confirming or modifying those predictions as needed. At this stage, students need to know how to self-monitor and regulate their reading; for example, students recognize when they encounter difficulty, identify the source of the difficulty, and determine which strategy to use to overcome the difficulty. Through explicit strategy instruction, students will acquire a repertoire of skills such as knowing how to adjust their reading rate to fit the demands of the selection and their reading purposes, focus on word meanings, change their predictions, ask questions, or go back and reread. This chapter will examine a number of ways that teachers can continue to assist students in their comprehension beyond before-reading strategies and into during-reading strategies for different texts.

You're the Expert

1. How do you model during-reading strategies to students?

2. Using a variety of texts, how can you assist students in figuring out the main idea of texts as they read?

3. Select three reading passages for students that they have not yet read. Allow students to read one passage on their own and another with a partner. Read aloud the third passage to the class. Ask students what strategies they used to determine the meaning of each passage and which one they prefer.

During reading, students need to become actively engaged with the text. Good readers know how and when to use certain reading strategies. Students can monitor their comprehension by paying attention to what does and does not make sense in a text. This may mean rereading a part of the selection, asking a classmate or the teacher a question, or consulting an expert source such as a dictionary. Throughout the reading process, teachers should encourage students to have a clearly defined purpose, anticipate what will happen next, and make predictions. It is important for teachers to help students to become aware of their metacognitive strategies for reading. Students need to think about how they think as they read.

At Your Fingertips

When reading any particular text, students need to employ several strategies. Teachers need to engage students in the reading task and model appropriate strategies. Some general guidelines you should offer your students include the following:

1. Connecting (i.e., making connections with people, places, situations, and ideas they know)

2. Finding meaning (i.e., determining what the author is saying about people, places, situations, and ideas)

3. Questioning (i.e., paying attention to those words, ideas, and actions that may be unclear, keeping in mind that they may become clear later)

4. Making and confirming predictions (i.e., trying to figure out what will happen and verifying it in the text)

5. Making inferences (i.e., determining the author's intent by reading between the lines and inferring what the author does not actually say)

6. Reflecting and evaluating (i.e., responding to what they have read and making judgments)

Active reading requires students to apply their background knowledge to the reading, interact with the selections, become imaginatively and intellectually involved, and share and shape their responses within the classroom setting. Teachers can help students read selections more effectively by getting them actively involved in the reading process, guiding the reading process with questions and activities that help them build their own understanding of what they are reading, and modeling the strategies that effective readers use as they read.

Helping Students Become Involved with Text

Reading does not have to be limited to subject-matter texts. The way you read passages can also be varied for students. By offering a number of different reading formats, teachers can actively engage their students in reading.

Choral Reading

One preferred way to build students' reading confidence, improve fluency, and nurture a classroom community is by reading selections aloud as an entire class at a moderate rate. Typically, a teacher will tell students, "Keep your voice with mine." By having students read along with classmates and the teacher, they are hearing a fluent reading of the passage and are assisted in making meaning as they read. Students may also silently read material before choral reading. Preferably, teachers will allow students to repeat readings in order to engage them further.

Echo Choral Reading

There are several ways in which choral reading can be done. Another favorite is echo choral reading. Here the teacher (or a fluent reader) reads the assigned text phrase by phrase or sentence by sentence with appropriate expression and meaning. The students in the class then echo the reader's voice after each phrase or sentence, rereading the words in the text and attempting to duplicate the meaningful expression provided by the reader. Students need to be reminded to track the text carefully with their eyes during echo reading. The temptation is simply to echo without reading. Students need to follow along visually because they may be asked to read the same text on their own at a later time.

Paired Reading

Paired reading is a form of choral reading done with two readers. Usually, one reader is more fluent than the other. The two students read together, one pointing to the text as it is read. The less able reader will benefit from the support of the more fluent partner. The less able reader may choose to try to go solo by signaling to his or her partner (often a tap of the finger will suffice) that he or she wants to read without assistance. The more able reader follows along silently and jumps in with his or her voice whenever the less able reader begins having difficulty. Research by Topping (1987) has demonstrated the positive impact of paired reading on comprehension.

Partner Reading

In partner reading, the teacher asks students to whisper-read to their partners. Students may alternate by sentence, paragraph, page, or time (e.g., five minutes). The student who is not reading acts as a coach who corrects any reading errors. One of the most successful ways to use partner reading is by pairing better readers with struggling readers. Using this format, the first reader (better reader) reads material, and the second reader reads the same material. Afterward, both students read the material together.

Audio-Assisted Reading

Choral, paired, and partner reading provide assistance to less able readers while they read by providing an oral reading model who reads with them. It may not always be possible to provide a live person to read with the less able readers. An alternative is to provide students with a tape, CD, or computer recording of the passage. The reader receives the same assistance as in choral and paired reading, reading the text while simultaneously hearing a fluent rendering of the same passage. Prerecorded materials can easily be purchased at bookstores or through school book clubs. Teachers can also make them. Even better is to have students produce these "talking books" for one another. Research on the impact of audio-assisted reading, or what Marie Carbo has called "talking books," is compelling (Carbo 1978, 1981; Pluck 1995).

Cloze Reading

Students who better understand key vocabulary words comprehend more of what they read. One way to encourage students to interact with text is to read selections and pause on "meaningful" words. Students can read the deleted words and predict word meanings based on context. This activity tends to boost students' fluency as well.

Silent Reading

Teachers can use silent reading successfully with students on their own and in small groups. By posing prereading questions, teachers give students something specific to think about as they read. Be sure to remind students to think about what they are reading because they will be discussing the passage after all students have read it. Teachers may even ask students to jot notes (use sticky notes that can be placed on the page itself) that reflect their thoughts, questions, wonderings, and ideas about their reading. These notes can be referred to during the discussion following the reading.

Some teachers like to tell students to read a certain amount and to reread material if they finish early. The teacher will monitor students' reading by asking students to whisper-read and tell the teacher what they are thinking about as they read.

Building Comprehension Through Questioning

Asking students questions during reading has proven effective in improving students' comprehension (National Reading Panel 2000; Morrow and Gambrell 2001). Additionally, encouraging students to ask themselves questions as they read can greatly assist them in comprehending what they read.

Teachers can use the questions provided in the manuals accompanying the reading program they are using. However, teachers often spark greater interest among students when they and their students collaborate to generate their own questions about the texts they are reading. When formulating questions, teachers should always consider the reading skills of their students, the content of the text, and what the students need to understand. According to Ciardiello (1998), these questions may vary from recall questions (e.g., Who? What? When? Where?) and convergent-thinking questions (e.g., Why? How? In what ways…?) to divergent-thinking questions (e.g., Imagine…? Suppose…? Predict…? If…then…?) and evaluative-thinking questions (e.g., Can you defend…? How would you judge…? How would you justify…? What do you think…?).

Name That Question

One way to generate interest among students in asking different types of questions is to create a pyramid of types of questions. (Teachers can classify these questions in a variety of ways using the examples above. Straight-recall questions would be on the bottom, while evaluative-thinking questions would be at the top.) Questions that require students to make inferences or educated guesses about the passage would be in the middle. Challenge students to ask themselves different types of questions as they read, and reward students who can ask the most varied types of questions and questions that require the most critical thinking with bonus reading time. Involving students in creating this pyramid provides opportunities for them to explore different forms of questions and recognize the kinds of thinking necessary to answer various types of questions.

Questioning the Author

Active reading involves students in creating dialogue with the author by striving to reformulate what the author is saying and then extending it. This involvement encourages students to concentrate and think about what they are reading. Questioning the author (McKeown, Beck, and Worthy 1993) allows students to identify the author's intent and evaluate how well the author communicates that intent. Students read a selection of text and answer questions such as the following: What is the author trying to tell you? Why is the author telling you that? Does the author say it clearly? How could the author have said things more clearly? What would you say instead? This approach shifts students' attention from trying to understand the text to observing what the author does to make the text understandable. Sometimes writers do not express themselves clearly, and it is valuable for students to pick up on that and consider changes that would improve the expression.

Think-Alouds

Another effective way to teach students how to make sense of text is for teachers to demonstrate how they make associations. Teacher think-alouds are one of the most effective strategies teachers employ to demonstrate the use of reading strategies to students while reading. By vocalizing how they infer, reread, create visual images, check predictions, and adjust their reading rate to match purpose and material, teachers can model for students the value of self-talk while reading.

Think-alouds work particularly well during the read-aloud period when the teacher shares a favorite story. You may stop occasionally throughout the reading to share what is happening in your own mind as you are reading. Be sure to ask students to share what they are thinking as they listen to you read.

Monitoring Comprehension

Comprehension strategies are used "to relate ideas in a text to what they already know; to keep track of how well they are understanding what they read; and when understanding breaks down, to identify what is causing the problem and how to overcome it" (Lehr and Osborn 2005). In order to summarize and determine the main idea of what they read, good readers know how to apply a number of strategies.

Check Me Out

As they read, students should monitor how much they understand. One way they can do this is by asking themselves questions such as, Does this make sense? If it does not make sense, encourage students to use a fix-up strategy (e.g., reread, look back, read ahead, restate in their own words).

Stay On Target (a.k.a. Margin Notes)

Many teachers are familiar with struggling readers whose primary difficulty with comprehension rests on their focus. When students' thoughts drift away from the text, they need to become more active with the text by reading a paragraph at a time and writing items in the margin, such as the main idea, their inferences, and whether they agree or disagree with a point the author makes. It takes most students only a few paragraphs of margin notes to get them refocused on the text.

K I S S (Keep It Simple, Silly)

Anyone who has ever had to clean out a garage can attest that large tasks can seem insurmountable. The solution is to break up the task into smaller pieces. This idea works well for students who appear overwhelmed with a particular book. Chunking the passage into smaller segments makes the task more manageable. To find the answers to their questions, encourage students to read only a short section, one paragraph to one page, depending on the difficulty of the text. In order for students to determine the "big idea" of what they are reading, they must first master putting together the little ideas. Scaffolding students' reading in this way provides the support they need to actively think as they read.

Making Inferences

For students to comprehend what they read, they must be able to connect with a text as they read it. They make connections in three ways: text to self (i.e., relating text to their own prior experiences); text to text (i.e., relating what they read to other items that they have read); and text to world (i.e., relating text to worldly events). (More ideas about these connections are provided in Chapter 9.) Not all information is explicitly stated within the text, and good readers fill in the gaps by using all of their senses to determine what the author is saying. In expository (nonfiction) text, visualizing is most beneficial, while narrative (storytelling) texts tend to engage all of the students' senses, especially their emotions.

Graphic Organizers

The main effect of graphic organizers appears to be on the improvement of the reader's ability to remember the content that has been read (Harris and Hodges 1995). Graphic organizers help students represent content graphically, organize ideas to show the relationships among them, and support students' memory of the content that they have read. When mapping, students create a visual representation of material (these maps typically include headings and subheadings with shapes drawn around each one and important supporting details written below each shape). Good readers use graphic organizers to enhance comprehension.

Reader Breather

Many students become overwhelmed by what they are reading, especially with highly informative texts. To make comprehension of such texts less daunting, encourage students to occasionally stop reading, reflect on concepts and ideas that have just been introduced, make connections to their background experiences, and seek clarification. This is called a "reader breather," or three-minute pause (Wiggins and McTighe 1998).

Paint a Picture

Students must realize that reading is an active, cognitive process involving more than physically looking at the printed words. It involves looking at the meanings and ideas behind those words. As students read, they visualize what they read.

Sketch to Stretch

Prompt students to develop pictures and images in their head as they read. Better yet, have them sketch on paper the images that emerge in their minds as they read. Later, these images can be the basis for discussion of the text itself. In one version of this strategy, called Sketch to Stretch (Rasinski and Padak 2004), students share their sketches one at a time with their classmates and allow their classmates to talk about each student's sketch. The student who drew the sketch does not talk. During the discussion, the students share their own insights and attempt to determine the main idea the student artist was attempting to convey through the sketch. At the end of the discussion, the student who made the sketch provides his or her own interpretation of the drawing. The process of creating and responding to the images made by readers requires students to dig deep into meaning—meaning on the page and meaning that the readers infer from the passage.

Journals

Students need practice with thinking through literary texts as they read. Keeping a journal in which they respond to the literature in terms of what they think or how they feel about what they are reading gives students and teachers insights into how students are building meaning as they read. A double-entry journal allows students to jot down notes, quotations, and comments as they read (i.e., their initial response) on the left side of the page. After reading and possibly rereading a text, they can write more extensive responses on the right side of the page. This combination of writing and thinking encourages readers to focus on the meaning. And, when they share their journal entries with one another, students have the opportunity to discover how other readers made meaning from the same text.

Guided-Reading Procedure

After a purpose for reading has been set, students read an assignment to remember as much as possible. Next, they brainstorm everything they can remember, individually or with a partner. They check the text for additional information and correct any inaccuracies. Finally, they organize their recollections into an outline, semantic map, or summary. This step-by-step procedure leads students through the process of making meaning as they read.

Jigsaws

The jigsaw strategy is an effective cooperative learning strategy that enables students to extend their comprehension abilities as well as helping them to reflect on how they worked as a group (Erwin 2004; Slavin 1994). All students read a common selection. Students are divided into groups and each group is given a specific responsibility (e.g., Group 1: Rephrase the article in your own words; Group 2: Identify questions that you would like to ask the author; Group 3: Elaborate on the implications/consequences of the author's position; Group 4: What assumptions is the author making? Evaluate these assumptions; Group 5: What information does the author present and what else would you like to know?).

Each group has a different part of the puzzle. Then, new groups are formed with each group having at least one member from the previous five groups. In the new groups, each member adds to the discussion by sharing his or her part of the jigsaw. Ideally, a jigsaw discussion results in complete and comprehensive coverage of the article, in which all group members take an essential role.

Directed Reading-Thinking Activity

Students examine the first portion of a selection and make predictions about the topic or plot. Then they silently read the first portion, stopping at a preselected place just prior to an important event. Students confirm or modify their first predictions and continue stopping at various preselected places.

What Do Good Readers Do as They Read?

Students need to actively engage with text as they read. Teachers can model a variety of strategies good readers use as they read in order to determine the main idea of a passage, summarize it, and make inferences. By constantly asking themselves questions and visualizing text, students are more likely to comprehend what they read. Chapter 9 specifically addresses what comprehension strategies students can use after they read a text.

Comprehension does not occur only after reading when a reader has the opportunity to ponder what has been read. Good readers make meaning while they read by stopping at various points within the text to ponder, question, make connections to other texts or to one's own life, create mental images, share with others, make judgments about the content, and make predictions about what may happen next in the text. The strategies presented in this chapter are simply ways to get novice readers to engage in the same sort of meaning making that all good readers do while reading.

Good readers are actively engaged with text and constantly refer to their background knowledge in order to better understand what they are reading. Additionally, they:

- try to guess what is coming next (i.e., anticipation)

- create mental pictures as they read (i.e., visualization)

- read with automaticity (i.e., they are fluent readers who focus their reading attention on comprehending what they read, not sounding out individual words)

- exhibit broad vocabularies and determine meanings of new vocabulary words through a variety of strategies (e.g., comprehending through context)

- make text-to-self, text-to-text, and text-to-world connections

- determine the most important information in any given passage (i.e., main idea)

- can summarize what they read

- ask questions as they read
- make inferences based on information in text and their prior experiences
- analyze what they read (i.e., read critically)

Chapter 9

Comprehension Strategies for After Reading

Felicia had just finished reading Peggy Rathman's Officer Buckle and Gloria, *the entertaining and heartwarming story of a police safety officer and his best friend, a police dog by the name of Gloria. Until Gloria became his partner, Officer Buckle's safety talks in schools tended to put students to sleep. However, once Gloria began to accompany Buckle on his presentations, students began to take notice. They found his talks most interesting. Officer Buckle thought he had finally hit his stride. Little did he know that his best friend Gloria was mocking Buckle behind his back while he gave his talks. During one of his best speeches, Officer Buckle noticed Gloria acting out in front of the students. Officer Buckle was deeply hurt by the actions of his best friend. The story shifts to how Buckle and Gloria make up and patch their friendship.*

After reading the book to herself, Felicia took her literature response journal out of her desk and without any prompting from her teacher, spent the next five minutes writing in her journal. Later that day, she allowed the teacher to read what she had written. In her entry for that day, Felicia wrote a brief summary of the book, and then described how she once had felt betrayed by someone she thought was her best friend. She explained how she and her friend were able to regain their friendship through an apology, an explanation, and an acceptance of the apology.

Without uttering a word or answering one question, Felicia demonstrated her comprehension of what she had read. Moreover, she had deepened her understanding of the book by making a personal connection between the events in the book and events from her own life. The analysis of both events required her to think deeply about and connect the meaning Rathman tried to portray in the story with a somewhat similar event that occurred in her own life. The analysis that went into that connection between text and life led to deep understanding—much deeper than a student simply providing an event-by-event summary of the story itself.

You're the Expert

Comprehension is taught before, during, and after reading. How is it that reading comprehension can occur after a reader has already read a text? What does a reader do after reading that fosters comprehension? In the example above, how can we say that comprehension is fostered when Felicia connects what she has read to something that occurred in her own life when the events from her life do not describe anything that actually occurred in the book?

At Your Fingertips

Having readers respond in meaningful ways to what they have read can foster reading comprehension. Consider the following questions:

1. In what ways do you respond to texts that you have read? Make a list of all the ways that you react to what you read after reading.

2. Ask another person how he or she often responds to various types of texts—stories or narratives? newspaper or informational articles? poetry and songs? materials that you read as part of a group—either in a place of worship, as a sports team, or as part of some other organization in which community reading or chanting is prevalent?

3. How have each of these responses helped you or another person gain a deeper understanding of what has been read? Which responses seem to be more effective in promoting understanding of a text? Which responses seem to be more engaging or entertaining for students? Which appear to be least effective when working with students? Why do you think so?

This chapter explores ways in which teachers can have students respond meaningfully to what they read—ways to teach and nurture comprehension *after* reading. Teachers will find approaches to post-reading response that are more conventional. We also present approaches that are somewhat less conventional, but equally, if not more, effective in getting readers to think deeply about, explore, and extend the meaning of the texts that they read. As you read and reflect on these strategies, think about how you have used these strategies in your own reading.

Post-Reading Discussions

Perhaps the most common way that teachers help students explore the meaning of a passage they have read is by encouraging them to talk about the passage with other students and perhaps the teacher. Many readers have similar experiences in their life through memberships in neighborhood book clubs, Bible-study groups, study groups at school, or simply talking about passages they thought were interesting and provocative with friends. Through the process of talking about the passage with others, sharing perspectives, and hearing the perspective of others, a reader is able to gain a deeper understanding of the passage.

In schools, reading discussions have traditionally been teacher-led, usually in one direction: the teacher asks a question and a student is called on to answer the question. Moreover, the questions that were asked tended to be the literal-level questions that could be answered by simply referring to information directly in the text: What were the names of the characters? Where did this story take place? Not much in the way of deep and thoughtful analysis occurs in such a discussion. Indeed, the major purpose of such discussions was more for the teacher to retain control over students and to check whether they had actually read the passage.

Fortunately, over the past two decades, the reading field has made major advances in the structure and dynamics of reading discussions. Discussions have become more authentic, more like the kinds of discussions that occur when a group of adults sit down to talk about a shared book or other reading. Whether this new form of discussion is called a literature discussion group, book club, book bistro, or some other interesting name, the aim of the activity is to give students an authentic forum and structure for discussing meaning. Students answer questions, and they also ask questions. The questions should go well beyond the literal level. Students can ask and respond to questions that ask for their opinions and thoughts on various aspects of the passage, from the actual content, character analysis, organization, literary style of the author, word choice, and illustrations.

Since students may not be familiar with how discussions actually run, some teachers find it helpful to assign specific roles to students before the reading begins. Each student makes a contribution to the discussion by asking questions about and providing thoughtful responses to questions about the specific area assigned. Here are just a few assigned roles that can work well when getting started with literature discussion groups (Daniels 2002):

- Discussion leader—leads the discussion and encourages participation by all students
- Summarizer—begins the discussion with a summary of the reading
- Text-to-life connector—shares and discusses text-to-life connections found in the passage
- Text-to-text connector—shares and discusses text-to-text connections
- Questioner—finds and shares interesting and provocative questions that emerge from the passage
- Imaginer—leads a discussion of interesting images in the passage
- Predictor—leads a discussion about possible upcoming events in the next section of the text
- Architect—examines the structure of the passage; comments on and asks questions about the clarity and underlying structure of the text (e.g., chronological order, list structure, compare-contrast, problem-solution, etc.)

- Sentence finder/word wizard—finds and leads a discussion of interesting sentences and words found in the passage
- Critic—provides an overall evaluation of the passage: Was it worth reading? He or she asks classmates to give a thumbs-up or thumbs-down on the piece.

What other roles could be added to a literature discussion group structure? The roles for students rotate from one reading and discussion to another. As students become more comfortable in the ways that discussions are run, teachers may ease students out of specific roles and ask them to simply use their experiences from these more structured discussions to engage in more open-ended and authentic discussions.

Text-to-Self Connections

While reading the previous section about literature discussions, you were asked to think about times in your life when you engaged in authentic literature discussions. Hopefully, as you thought about your own experiences with text discussions, your understanding of the points made in that section became clearer. This is an example of a text-to-self connection (TS), a powerful strategy for moving readers to think about their own experiences that are similar in some way to the ones portrayed in a text.

TS connections are relatively easy to bring into classroom discussions. Although younger students may make TS connections that are superficial and not thoughtfully analyzed, with practice (and modeling by the teacher), students become more adept at making such connections on their own. A result of the connection and the subsequent analysis that occurs with the TS connection is that students achieve a deeper level of meaning.

As students read a text, simply prompt them to think about how an event in the text, a character, a setting, or some other element of a text is similar to something they may have experienced in their own lives. Later, when discussing (or writing) about the reading, ask students to describe the connections they made and discuss the extent to which their own personal experiences were similar to or different than those portrayed in the reading. You may want to use a graphic organizer such as a Venn diagram to help students organize their thinking. A T-chart in which students list events or elements from the text on one side and corresponding events from their own lives on the other side is also a good way to organize students' thinking and guide their oral (or written) discussion of the text.

Text-to-Text Connections

Readers often find themselves thinking about how the book or passage they are reading is similar to another text they have previously read. They may even find themselves doing a bit of analysis of both passages: how the two passages are alike and how they are different. This strategy of making connections to other texts and exploring the meaning of both is often called a text-to-text connection (TT). Like TS connections, TT connections are an effective vehicle for nurturing students' reading comprehension and moving students to deeper levels of textual analysis and understanding.

During the process of reading a passage, ask students to keep in mind a passage they have previously read. This should be one that the teacher knows is good for comparing and contrasting with the text being read. Just recently, second-grade students in Sally Witzen's room were reading Jon Scieszka's *The True Story of the Three Little Pigs.* As students began to read, Mrs. Witzen prompted students to think about how the story they were currently reading was both similar to and different from the traditional story of *The Three Little Pigs* they had heard many times before and had read the previous week.

Once students had finished reading, Mrs. Witzen provided pairs of students with a three-column chart and asked them to put the traditional tale of *The Three Little Pigs* in one column and Scieszka's story in the second column. Then each pair made a listing of the various events and elements that were present in both stories in the first two columns. In the third column, they wrote an analysis of how those events were either alike or different. Students then used the study guide they had created to engage in a brief discussion of the story and added to their guide as they heard other pairs of students report the findings of their analyses. They also wrote a brief compare-and-contrast essay on the book using the analyses sheet as the basis for their written response.

TT connections can be used in much the same was as TS connections. The teacher simply needs to prompt students before and during reading to keep another previously read text in mind as they read (the prompting may also occur after the reading so that students begin their analyses after having read the text). After reading, students use the TS connections for talking and writing (and thinking) more deeply about the story they have just read. As students become more adept at making TT connections and analyses, they can be asked to choose the other text or texts used for the connection.

Text-to-World Connections

Like TS and TT connections, making text-to-world connections (TW) involves students in comparing and contrasting (i.e., analyzing and thinking deeply about) a passage they have just read with events that have occurred outside of their own immediate lives and outside another text they have previously read. Students are asked to make their analyses broader. The TW connection is perhaps the most common connection used in school, especially in other areas of the curriculum. When reading a chapter on the American Revolution, students may be asked to connect that war with the War of 1812, the American Civil War, or the French Revolution. When reading and studying the civil rights movement in America, students may be prompted by their teacher to compare that era in history with apartheid in South Africa. Teachers know that the analysis in which students identify similarities and differences leads to deep levels of understanding and insight.

TW connections are employed in much the same way as TS and TT connections. The teacher chooses an event from present times or history and asks students to analyze that event in light of what they have just read. The TW connection becomes the basis for furthering the meaningful interaction with the text as students discuss their analyses with other classmates or write about their analyses in summary or essay form.

Compare and Contrast

TS, TT, and TW connections are all forms of compare and contrast that are helpful in moving students to deeper levels of comprehension, well beyond literal comprehension. There are other forms of compare and contrast. Indeed, teachers often use compare and contrast as a teaching tool. How often have you used the word *like* to explain something to your students? Teachers will often teach something new by describing how the new concept is *like* and unlike something they know from their own previous experiences. Through that discussion and shared analysis, students gain an understanding of the new concept the teacher had intended to present.

Graphic organizers or visual displays are particularly effective devices for helping students make compare and contrast analyses between two or more reading passages, other events, concepts, or ideas that a teacher may want students to analyze. Compare-and-contrast grids are one of the most effective ways to promote compare-and-contrast analysis.

In a compare-and-contrast grid, the passages or elements within one or more passages (e.g., characters) are horizontally in the top row of cells. Along the left-hand column are the questions or prompts for analyzing the elements on the top row. Elements in both the top row and left column can either be selected in advance by answering the teacher questions or brainstormed by the student or group of students. Once the top row and left column are complete, students engage in analyzing elements in the top row by the questions in the left column. Students' responses are written in the appropriate cell. An example of a compare-and-contrast grid is provided on the following page.

Figure 9.1: Compare-and-Contrast Grid of Significant American Poets

	Shel Silverstein	Walt Whitman	Emily Dickinson	Robert Frost
Topics of the poet's work?				
Poetic and literary devices used?				
Poet's intent or purpose for writing?				
Main audience for the poet's work?				
Significance of the poet's work today? for yourself and your friends? in the future? Why do you think so?				

Students would need to think deeply in order to provide a reasonable response to the questions for the various poets listed. Moreover, not all students' responses would be the same. The questions posed are more inferential and critical than literal. Students are asked to give their own reasoned opinions about the poets, not simply provide literal information that can be lifted directly from the work of the poets themselves.

Once the grid is complete, students can use the grid as a guide for a rich and authentic conversation about the poets with classmates. They can also use the guide for writing detailed summaries, analyses, and essays on the poets presented in the grid. In all cases, the grid itself helps to move students into deeper levels of meaning after they have read several works by the poets mentioned.

Written Responses—Summaries, Syntheses, Essays, and More

Earlier in this chapter, it was noted that discussion with others is a way to deepen a student's comprehension of a text that they have read. Sometimes readers can have internal discussions that can lead to deeper understandings of their reading. Have you ever found yourself mulling over something you have read, thinking it through, reconsidering your initial reactions to the text, but not necessarily sharing this experience with someone else? You mulled it over or thought it through on your own. That process of thinking something through with yourself, or having an internal discussion, can be a very effective way to deepen comprehension. How can teachers get students to engage in that internal dialogue that leads to deeper comprehension?

Having students write responses to their reading is an excellent way to engage them in an internal discussion. Before writing, students need to consider what they wish to write; in other words, they need to mull over the passage they have just read. Good writing requires the writer to think before putting pen to paper.

Summaries

Summaries are a simple but effective way to promote internal analysis. A summary is simply a restatement of the information from a passage in a compact form. Summaries require a reader to think about the main points in a reading passage and organize or structure those main points in a logical manner so that a reader of a written summary can understand the nature and intent of the original passage.

Although the concept of a summary is itself easy to understand, writing good summaries can be quite challenging. Perhaps the best way to teach summarization is for teachers to model the process for students, and while developing a summary in front of students, discuss the process itself. Among the key points in developing a summary are the following activities:

- Identify key words and bits of information from a text. Restate this information in your own words in notes or on note cards.

- Examine and prioritize the information you have collected. Delete information that under second analysis is redundant or not important.

- Organize the remaining notes into logical groups. Provide a label or descriptor for each group.

- Organize the various groups into a logical order.

- Write a summary of the passage you have read. Try to retell the major points of the text using your organized and ordered notes.

The process described above may not be the exact procedure that everyone follows in developing a summary, but it does provide a model for teachers to use with their students. While modeling this process for students, and while students engage in their own summary writing, both teachers and students have to engage in a thoughtful analysis of the passage.

Synthesis—A Summary of Summaries

A synthesis is a single summary of multiple texts or other information sources. The process of doing a synthesis is more complex than writing a summary of a single text; consequently, a more complex form of comprehension is required.

The process of writing a synthesis, however, is much the same as writing a summary. Here is the general process:

- Create summaries of various texts that were read. Identify the main idea of each text and restate the main idea in notes or on note cards.

- Examine and prioritize the information you have collected. Delete information that under second analysis is redundant or not important.

- Organize the remaining notes into logical groups. Provide a label or descriptor for each group.

- Organize the various groups into a logical order.
- Write a synthesis of the passages you have read. Try to retell the major points of the texts using your organized and ordered notes.

As with summary writing, learning to analyze multiple texts and write syntheses is best done under the guidance of a teacher who models the process and, through his or her own modeling and concurrent discussion, makes the process as visible as possible for students.

Essays

Essays can be considered another form of summarization; however, they differ from summaries and syntheses in that the writer presents a particular point of view. In an essay, the writer attempts to make a point using information that often comes from one or more textual sources. The writing of an essay involves analysis, speculation, and interpretation, all of which are comprehension processes that lead a reader and writer to deeper levels of understanding.

In school, essays are usually assignments given by a teacher to students (e.g., compare and contrast the work of two authors; after reading a newspaper article on universal health care, write an essay for or against the need for government-mandated health insurance for all Americans; write a critique of the most recent winner of the Newbery Award). Writing a good essay requires a solid understanding of the topic, information from the text as well as other sources, and the student's own background knowledge. Orchestrating all that information into a thoughtful, coherent, and compelling essay requires students to dig deep into meaning.

As with summaries and syntheses, the ability to write essays evolves over time and with a lot of guided practice. First students need to read, think about, and discuss already-written essays by other students. They need to see their teacher involved in the process of writing an essay, and finally, they need to try their own hand at writing essays on a regular basis. They need to read their classmates' own essays, critique them, and allow their own work to be analyzed by others.

Similar to reading comprehension itself, through the process of writing and responding to writing, students develop an understanding of how essays work, including the process of developing an essay—a process that itself develops students' comprehension.

Open Response

Nearly any type of writing in response to reading will promote deep thinking and comprehension about what was read. Many teachers have students keep written logs, journals, or notebooks in which they write daily responses to what they read. Sometimes the teacher defines the response (e.g., Summarize today's reading. Predict what will happen in the next chapter. What literary devices did the author use in the passage today?).

In other cases, the written response will be left up to the student. The student is allowed to write whatever he or she may wish, as long as it has something to do with their reading. Often students will write a personal, subjective response about how the reading made them feel, a personal connection to an event in their own lives, or a personal critique of the piece. These reflective responses also require readers to think about some aspect of what they read, to think more deeply about the passage, and then translate their thoughts into written words.

Then, when students share their open responses with one another, they discover how other students felt about and understood the reading. Students will discover other responses and other ways to approach written reflections. Open-ended responses are a fine balance to teacher-defined written responses. These open-ended activities enable students to gain more control over their own reading, as well as empowering them to think about and comprehend the text in ways they feel are most important and personally appropriate.

More Written Responses—Transformations

Written responses can also take on more creative forms—forms in which the writer transforms the text he or she has read into another written form or genre. Written transformations of this type are quite evident in the entertainment world. Often, script writers transform a novel into a dramatic script for theater or movie production. Shakespeare's *Romeo and Juliet*, for example, has been transformed many times for screen and stage, from more contemporary versions of the play to a hit Broadway musical. In the world of writing, writers themselves will often transform a story into another form by changing one element of that story. Bill Martin changed bears when he transformed his noted *Brown Bear, Brown Bear*, into *Panda Bear, Panda Bear*, and *Polar Bear, Polar Bear*. Dave Pilkey transformed Clement Moore's classic Christmas poem into a contemporary poem that celebrated a different holiday in *The Night Before Thanksgiving*. One of our favorite transformations occurred in John Scieszka's *The True Story of the Three Little Pigs*, where readers get to hear the wolf's side of the story. Jane Yolen's *Sleeping Ugly* is another example of transformative writing—a variation on the traditional *Sleeping Beauty* story with a surprising ending.

Although viewed as a writing method, such written transformations are seen as very high-level comprehension activities as well. In order to transform one text into another, the writer has to think deeply about the original text, explore what he or she wants to change, and how he or she wants to change it in his or her transformation. Such a process involves inferential comprehension, as the writer has to make educated guesses as to how a story may play itself out if one of the key features were altered.

Text transformations are ideal for student writers to develop their writing skills as they use the original text as a foundation or scaffold for their own writing. Such transformations also develop students' reading comprehension, as they challenge students to think deeply and creatively about the meaning they are trying to convey to readers of their own writing.

Text transformations can take a variety of forms. Below are some common suggestions for written text transformations:

- Prequels and sequels: Tell the story that occurred before or after the original story.

- Change the gender: What happens when the gender of the main character changes?

- Change the time: How does a story play out in a different time period?

- Change the location: What happens when a story that is originally set in the country is transplanted to a city, beach, or mall?

- Alter the problem or key focus of the original story in some form: Change a description of a very bad day into the description of a great day.

- Change the point of view: Try rewriting a story from another character's point of view. Write the story in the voice of that character.

- Change the genre or text type: Rewrite a story as a script, the lead in a story for a newspaper article, an advice column, a radio commercial, a narrative poem, a series of journal entries, etc.

The possibilities for text transformations are many and varied. The potential for students to discover deeper meaning is enormous. Consider the deep level of thinking that goes into students writing their own version of Judith Viorst's classic *Alexander and the Terrible, Horrible, No Good, Very Bad Day*, one of the books most often transformed by elementary students. Students who write their own versions of the book need to consider what makes for a bad day, often thinking about their own horrible days, and how a story about that day might be crafted. When students participate in such activities, they are engaging in very sophisticated levels of comprehension processing.

Other Transformations

When a text is transformed, the writer must think deeply about the meaning of the original text and the new text. The previous section gave examples of how these transformations might take place in writing. However, text transformations do not always have to take a written form. Texts can be transformed in other ways—other forms of representing experience. And, as with written transformations, readers who do such transformations must think deeply about how they are re-representing the meaning of the original text. The following ideas are some ways that students might transform texts they read into forms other than writing.

Visual Transformations

Perhaps the most common form of nonwritten transformations comes when teachers ask students to draw a picture of some part of a text they have read or perhaps draw a diagram or chart of the events of a story. Although common and rather simple, the act of making a visual representation of a passage requires readers to think deeply about the meaning embedded in the text. They need to choose a certain portion or episode in the text to portray, and they need to think about characters, setting and location, time, and the visual to be represented. Often in their drawings, students will have to add things that are not mentioned in the actual text: perhaps adding characters, structures, identifying the time of day, even selecting the colors used in the various parts of the drawing. All of these additions that were not specified in the original text are inferences, or educated guesses about events in a text. Inferential comprehension is one of the highest levels of comprehension, and in this case, it is done through the creation of a picture or the transformation of a written text into a visual form.

Sketch-to-Stretch is a specific approach for using visual representations to explore the meaning of a written passage (Rasinski and Padak 2004). In Sketch-to-Stretch, individual readers are asked to quickly draw a sketch that represents some aspect of a passage they have just read. Then, in small groups, each student shares his or her drawing with other group members. Rather than the student explaining his or her sketch, other students discuss the drawing, attempting to determine what the student was trying to convey through the sketch. Once individual students share their own thoughts, the original artist explains his or her own perspective on the piece. After one sketch is discussed in this manner, the other students in the group share their drawings using the same process of open-ended response followed by an explanation from the artist.

The process of drawing, the discussion by fellow students, and the explanation by the student who made the drawing are all activities that promote deep thinking and comprehension of a text. Students share their own thoughts on a passage in several ways, and they gain the perspective of their fellow students. Sketch-to-Stretch is a wonderful and creative way to engage students in exploring text meaning in a variety of ways.

Physical Transformations—Tableau

In physical transformations, students use parts of the physical world to re-represent the meaning of the text. The most immediate part of the physical world available to a student is his or her body. Tableau is a legitimate performing art in which actors represent or convey meaning with their bodies. However, unlike acting in which the performers can move and talk, tableau is a still life in which the actors depict a scene using their unmoving bodies, like statues. Often you see a tableau in theatrical plays at the beginning of acts or scenes in which the actors hold a pose for several seconds before moving.

Tableaux are very engaging and creative ways for students to transform and explore the meaning of a text they have read. Here is how a tableau might work in your classroom. After students have read a passage, ask them to work in small groups of three to five students to create a tableau that represents an important event within the text they have just read. In a matter of only a few minutes, the groups need to choose a scene, assign parts, and explore how each actor will position himself or herself in the actual tableau. All students in a group must be part of the tableau. If the scene requires three people and there are five students in the group, two students will have to take the roles of "extras," or props, such as trees, doors, or chairs.

Once all groups are ready (it should take no longer than five minutes to create a tableau), each individual group performs its tableau for the rest of the class. On the teacher's cue, the members of each tableau become statues in their assigned places and positions. Then for the next several minutes, members of the class attempt to determine the actual scene from the written text that is being portrayed in the tableau. Once one group has completed their performance, the other groups perform their tableaux in a similar manner.

The process of creating a tableau is a comprehension activity. In developing their tableaux, groups of students talk about the meaning of the text and how they will portray that meaning through their tableaux. Then when each tableau is being performed and the rest of the class is viewing, discussing, and determining the meaning of the tableau, comprehension—the exploration of textual meaning—is again being nurtured. Not only do tableaux offer effective and different ways to explore meaning, they are activities that students find engaging and enjoyable. And those students who are more gifted at using their bodies to explore meaning are allowed to shine through tableau performances.

A tableau can be extended in several ways. Once students are familiar with the tableau format, they can be prompted by the teacher to think about what their character might say or do if they were allowed to come alive for a few seconds. (Even students who play trees need to think about what they might say or the gesture or movement they might make if they came alive!). Then during their group's portrayal of a tableau, while students are standing perfectly still and quiet, the teacher can tap individual students in the tableau on the shoulder. This action signals students that they can come alive and either say a few words, make a few sounds, or make a gesture or body movement for only a few seconds. The additional information given by the sound or the movement may assist the rest of the class in determining the meaning of the tableau. The planning of what to do or say is again a method for making students think deeply and creatively about the meaning of the text they have read.

Digging Deep After Reading

Although many people may think that comprehension occurs as a student reads a passage, readers can often delve more deeply into meaning when they think about a text after reading the passage. This chapter has explored effective and creative ways teachers can assist their students in reaching greater depths in text meaning after they have already read a passage. As students continue to think over a passage and mix the information from a passage with their own knowledge and past experiences, students' comprehension takes new and deeper forms—from literal to inferential to critical to creative. Comprehension does not end with literal understandings of text. Deeper levels of meaning need to be explored. Teachers can help students dig deeper into textual meaning through what they ask students to do after reading.

References Cited

Anderson, R. C., and P. D. Pearson. 1984. A schema-theoretic view of basic processes in reading comprehension. In *Handbook of reading research,* ed. P. D. Pearson, R. Barr, M. L. Kamil, and P. Mosenthal, 255–91. New York: Longman.

Bandura, A. 1989. Human agency in social cognitive theory. *American Psychologist* 44: 1175–84.

Barone, D. 1990. The written responses of young children: Beyond comprehension to story understanding. *The New Advocate* 3: 49–56.

Baumann, J. F., and B. S. Bergeron. 1993. Story map instruction using children's literature: Effects on first graders' comprehension of central narrative elements. *Journal of Reading Behavior* 25 (4): 407–37.

Blachowicz, C., and P. J. Fisher. 2002. *Teaching vocabulary in all classrooms.* 2nd ed. Upper Saddle River, NJ: Merrill/Prentice Hall.

Brassell, D. 2007. *News flash! Newspaper activities to meet language-arts standards & differentiate instruction.* Peterborough, NH: Crystal Springs.

Brassell, D. 2007. Inspiring young scientists with great books. *The Reading Teacher* 60 (4): 336–42.

Brassell, D., and J. Flood. 2004. *Vocabulary strategies every teacher needs to know.* San Diego, CA: Academic Professional Development.

Carbo, M. 1978. Teaching reading with talking books. *The Reading Teacher* 32:267–73.

Carbo, M. 1981. Making books talk to children. *The Reading Teacher* 35:186–89.

Catron, R. M., and N. Wingenbach. 1986. Developing the gifted reader. *Theory into Practice* 25 (2): 134–40.

Ciardiello, A. V. 1998. Did you ask a good question today? Alternative cognitive and metacognitive strategies. *Journal of Adolescent & Adult Literacy* 42 (3): 210–19.

Clymer, T. 1968. What is "reading"? Some current concepts. In *Innovation and chance in reading instruction: Sixty-seventh Yearbook of the National Society of the Study of Education*, ed. H. M. Robinson. Chicago: University of Chicago Press.

Daniels, H. 2002. *Literature circles: Voice and choice in book clubs and reading groups.* 2nd ed. Portland, ME: Stenhouse.

Davis, A. 2007. *Teaching reading comprehension.* Toronto, ON: Thomson Nelson.

Duke, N. K. 2004. The case for informational text. *Educational Leadership* 61 (6): 40–44.

Duke, N. K., and V. S. Bennett-Armistead. 2003. *Reading and writing informational text in the primary grades: Research-based practices.* New York: Scholastic.

Erwin, J. C. 2004. *The classroom of choice: Giving students what they need and getting what you want.* Alexandria, VA: Association for Supervision and Curriculum Development.

Esquith, R. 2004. *There are no shortcuts.* New York: Anchor.

Gardner, H. 1993. *Frames of mind: The theory of multiple intelligences.* 10th ed. New York: Basic Books.

Guthrie, J. T., and K. E. Cox. 2001. Classroom conditions for motivation and engagement in reading. *Educational Psychology Review* 13 (3): 283–302.

Hancock, M. R. 1992. Literature response journals: Insights beyond the printed page. *Language Arts* 61:141–50.

Hansen, J., and P. D. Pearson. 1983. An instructional study: Improving the inferential comprehension of good and poor fourth-grade readers. *Journal of Educational Psychology* 75: 821–29.

Harris, T. L., and R. E. Hodges. 1995. *The literacy dictionary: The vocabulary of reading and writing*. Newark, DE: International Reading Association.

Howell, H. 1987. Language, literature and vocabulary development for gifted students. *The Reading Teacher* 40:500–504.

Keene, E. O., and S. Zimmermann. 1997. *Mosaic of thought: Teaching comprehension in a reader's workshop*. Portsmouth, NH: Heinemann.

Lehr, F., and J. Osborn. 2005. A focus on comprehension. Honolulu, HI: Pacific Resources for Education and Learning. Available at http://www.prel.org/products/re_/re_focuscomp.pdf

Manzo, A., and U. Manzo. 1990. *Content area reading: A heuristic approach*. Upper Saddle River, NJ: Merrill/Prentice Hall.

Marzano, R. J. 1991. Language, the language arts, and thinking. In *Handbook of research on teaching the English language arts*, ed. J. Flood, J. M. Jensen, D. Lapp, and J. R. Squire, 559–86. New York: MacMillan.

Mason, J., P. Herman, and K. Au. 1991. Children's developing knowledge of words. In *Handbook of research on teaching the English language arts*, ed. J. Flood, J. M. Jensen, D. Lapp, and J. R. Squire, 721–31. New York: MacMillan.

McIntosh, M. E. 1982. An historical look at gifted education as it related to reading programs for the gifted. [ED 244472]

McKeown, M. G., and I. L. Beck. 2003. Taking advantage of read-alouds to help children make sense of decontextualized language. In *On reading books to children*, ed. A. van Kleeck, S. A. Stahl, and E. B. Bauer, 159–76. Mahwah, NJ: Erlbaum.

McKeown, M. G., I. L. Beck, and M. J. Worthy. 1993. Grappling with text ideas: Questioning the author. *The Reading Teacher* 46:560–66.

Mehigan, K. 2005. The strategy toolbox: A ladder to strategic teaching. *The Reading Teacher* 58:552–66.

Meyer, B. J. F., and G. E. Rice. 1984. The structure of text. In *Handbook of reading research*, ed. P. D. Pearson, R. Barr, M. L. Kamil, and P. Mosenthal, 319–51. New York: Longman.

Morrow, L. M., and L. B. Gambrell. 2001. Literature-based instruction in the early years. In *Handbook of early literacy research*, ed. S. B. Neuman and D. K. Dickinson, 348–60. New York: Guilford.

Nagy, W. 1988. *Teaching vocabulary to improve reading comprehension*. Newark, DE: International Reading Association.

National Reading Panel. 2000. *Report of the National Reading Panel: Teaching children to read. Report of the subgroups*. Washington, DC: U.S. Department of Health and Human Services, National Institutes of Health.

Nelson-Herber, J. 1986. Expanding and refining vocabulary in content areas. *Journal of Reading* 28:626–33.

Nichols, M. 2008. *Talking about text: Guiding students to increase comprehension through purposeful talk*. Huntington Beach, CA: Shell Education.

Oczkus, L. 2003. *Reciprocal teaching at work: Strategies for improving reading comprehension*. Newark, DE: International Reading Association.

Ogle, D. 1986. K-W-L group instruction strategy. In *Teaching reading as thinking*, ed A. S. Palincsar, D. S. Ogle, B. F. Jones, and E. G. Carr. Alexandria, VA: Association for Supervision and Curriculum Development.

Palincsar, A. S., and A. L. Brown. 1984. Reciprocal teaching of comprehension-fostering and comprehension-monitoring activities. *Cognition and Instruction* 2:117–75.

Pearson, P. D., and N. K. Duke. 2002. Comprehension instruction in the primary grades. In *Comprehension instruction: Research-based best practices*, ed. C. C. Block and M. Pressley, 247–58. New York: Guilford.

Pluck, M. 1995. Rainbow reading programme: Using taped stories. *Reading Forum* 1:25–29.

Pressley, M. 2001. Comprehension instruction: What makes sense now, what might make sense soon. *Reading Online* 5 (2). Available at http://www.readingonline.org/articles/handbook/pressley/index.html (accessed September 2001)

Pressley, M. 2002. Metacognition and self-regulated comprehension. In *What research has to say about reading instruction*. 3rd ed. Ed. A. E. Farstrup and S. J. Samuels, 291–309. Newark, DE: International Reading Association.

Pressley, M., and D. Forrest-Pressley. 1985. Questions and children's cognitive processing. In *The psychology of questions*, ed. A. C. Graesser and J. B. Black, 277–96. Hillsdale, NJ: Erlbaum.

Pressley, M., C. J. Johnson, S. Symons, J. A. McGoldrick, and J. A. Kurita. 1989. Strategies that improve children's memory and comprehension of what is read. *Elementary School Journal* 89: 3–32.

Raphael, T. 1984. Teaching learners about sources of information for answering comprehension questions. *Journal of Reading* 27:303–11.

Rasinski, T. 2003. *The fluent reader.* Jefferson City, MO: Scholastic Publishers.

Rasinski, T., and N. Padak. 2004. *Effective reading strategies: Teaching children who find reading difficult.* 3rd ed. Columbus, OH: Merrill/Prentice Hall.

Rasinski, T., and N. Padak. 2005. *Three-minute reading assessments.* New York: Scholastic.

Scott, J., D. Jamieson-Noel, and M. Asselin. 2003. Vocabulary instruction throughout the school day in 23 Canadian upper-elementary classrooms. *The Elementary School Journal* 103 (3): 269–86.

Sibberson, F., and K. Szymusiak. 2003. *Still learning to read: Teaching students in grades 3–6.* Portland, ME: Stenhouse Publishers.

Slavin, R. E. 1994. *Cooperative learning: Theory, research, and practice.* Boston: Allyn & Bacon.

Stahl, S. A. 1986. Three principles of effective vocabulary instruction. *Journal of Reading* 29 (7): 662–68.

Stauffer, R. G. 1969. *Directing reading maturity as a cognitive process.* New York: Harper & Row.

Sternberg, R. J. 1998. Abilities are forms of developing expertise. *Educational Researcher* 27 (3): 11–20.

Tharp, R. G., and R. Gallimore. 1989. *Rousing minds to life: Teaching, learning, and schooling in social context.* New York: Cambridge University Press.

Tompkins, G. E. 2004. *Teaching writing: Balancing process and product.* 4th ed. Upper Saddle River, NJ: Merrill/Prentice Hall.

Topping, K. 1987. Paired reading: A powerful technique for parent use. *The Reading Teacher* 40:604–14.

Tovani, C. 2000. *I read it, but I don't get it: Comprehension strategies for adolescent readers.* Portland, ME: Stenhouse.

Van Tassel-Baska, J. L. 1986. Effective curriculum and instructional models for talented students. *Gifted Child Quarterly* 30: 164–69.

Van Tassel-Baska, J. L. 1998. *Comprehensive curriculum for the gifted learners.* Boston: Allyn and Bacon.

Vygotsky, L. 1978. *Mind in society: The development of higher psychological processes.* Boston: Harvard University Press.

Wiggins, G., and J. McTighe. 1998. *Understanding by design.* Alexandria, VA: Association for Supervision and Curriculum Development.

Zutell, J., and T. Rasinski. 1991. Training teachers to attend to their students' oral reading fluency. *Theory to Practice* 30:211–17.

Children's Literature Cited

Hobbs, W. 2007. *Crossing the wire*. New York: Harper Collins.

Martin, B. 1983. *Brown bear, brown bear, what do you see?* New York: Henry Holt & Co.

Martin, B. 1995. *Polar bear, polar bear, what do you see?* New York: Henry Holt & Co.

Martin, B. 2007. *Panda bear, panda bear, what do you see?* New York: Henry Holt & Co.

Pilkey, D. 2004. *Twas the night before Thanksgiving*. New York: Scholastic.

Rathman, P. 1995. *Officer Buckle and Gloria*. New York: G. P. Putnam's Sons.

Scieszka, J. 1992. *The stinky cheese man and other fairly stupid tales*. New York: Viking.

Scieszka, J. 1996. *The true story of the three little pigs*. New York: Puffin.

Sendak, M. 1963. *Where the wild things are*. New York: Harper & Row.

Tolkien, J. R. R. 2003. *The two towers: The lord of the rings, part 2*. Boston: Houghton Mifflin.

Viorst, J. 1987. *Alexander and the terrible, horrible, no good, very bad day*. New York: Aladdin.

Yolen, J. 1997. *Sleeping ugly*. New York: Putnam Juvenile.

Comprehension
That *Works*

L earn innovative, engaging reading strategies that will empower you to improve comprehension instruction with your students. These unique classroom-tested strategies integrate current research findings with real-life observations of diverse students in action. Learn why these comprehension strategies matter as well as how to introduce activities which tap into students' multiple intelligences.

Danny Brassell, Ph.D., is an associate professor in the Teacher Education Department at California State University, Dominguez Hills. A former teacher, Danny is a popular national presenter who speaks on topics ranging from literacy to technology. He is the founder of The Lazy Readers' Book Club website, author of *Readers for Life: The Ultimate Reading Fitness Guide*, and coauthor of *Vocabulary Strategies Every Teacher Needs to Know*. Danny has written over 40 articles for academic journals, magazines, newspapers, and book chapters, as well as textbooks.

Timothy Rasinski, Ph.D., is a professor of literacy education at Kent State University. He is the author of several best-selling books and numerous articles on reading education, word study, and reading fluency. He is a popular and frequent presenter at reading and literacy conferences nationwide. His research is cited by the National Reading Panel in the development of *Reading First*, and he is currently co-editor of the *Journal of Literacy Research*.

SEP 50264

SHELL
EDUCATION

SEP 50264
Comprehension
That Works:
Taking Students
Beyond Ordinary
$29.99

ISBN 978-1-4258-0264-6
52999

9 781425 802646